Ante Timmermans

Musée Jenisch
Vevey

jrp|ringier

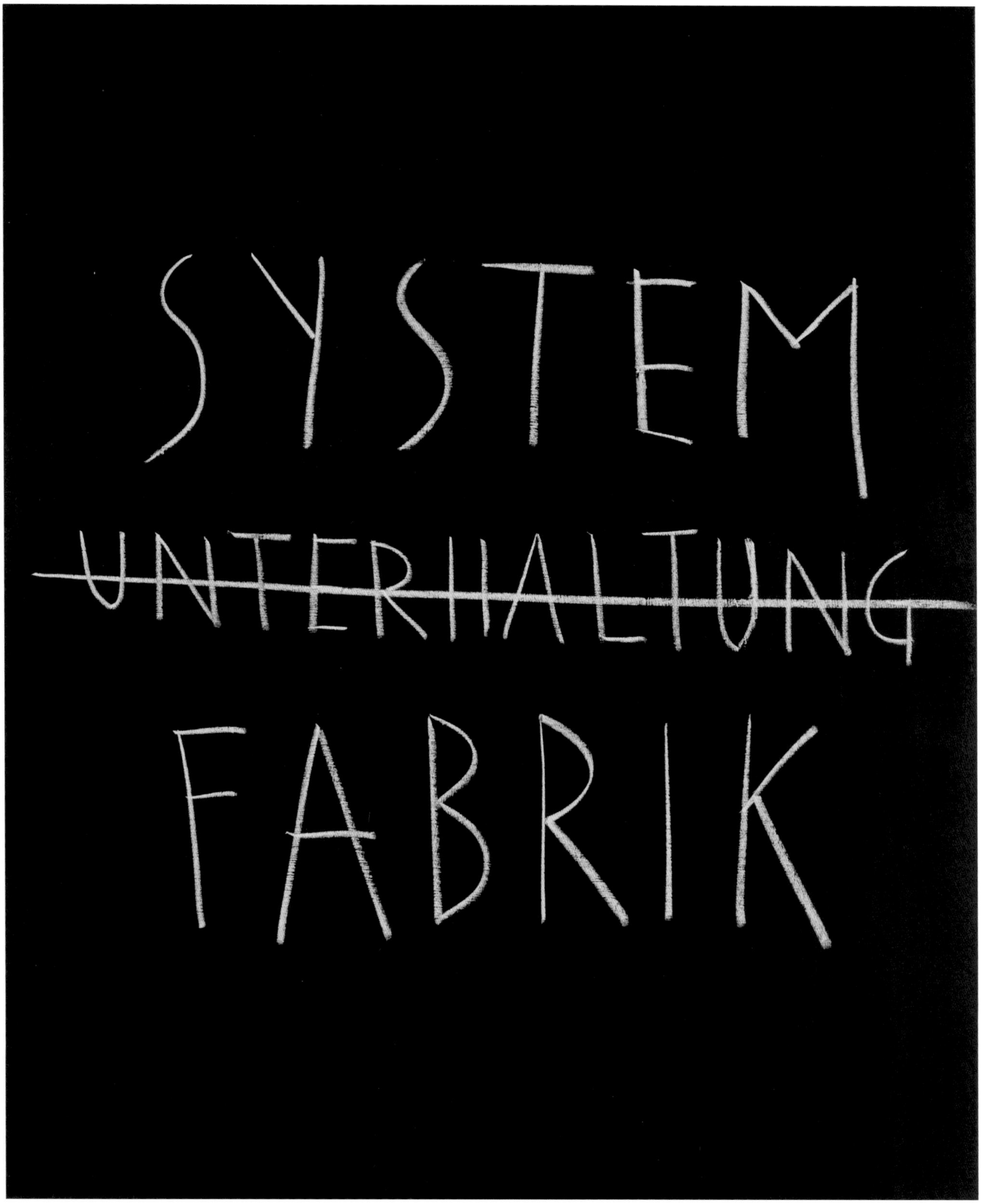

#22/2009 (UNTITLED), 2009

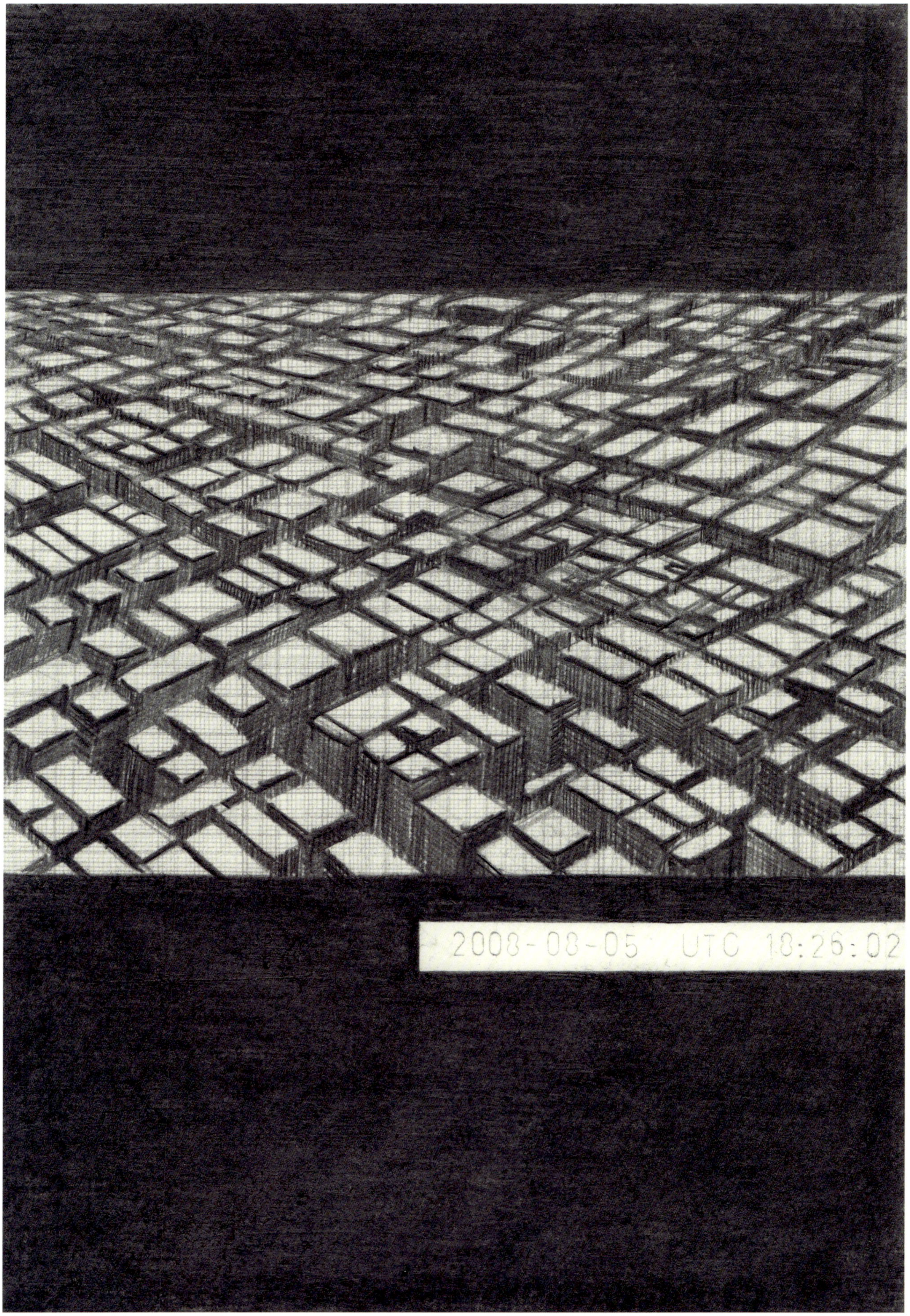

398/2008, 2008

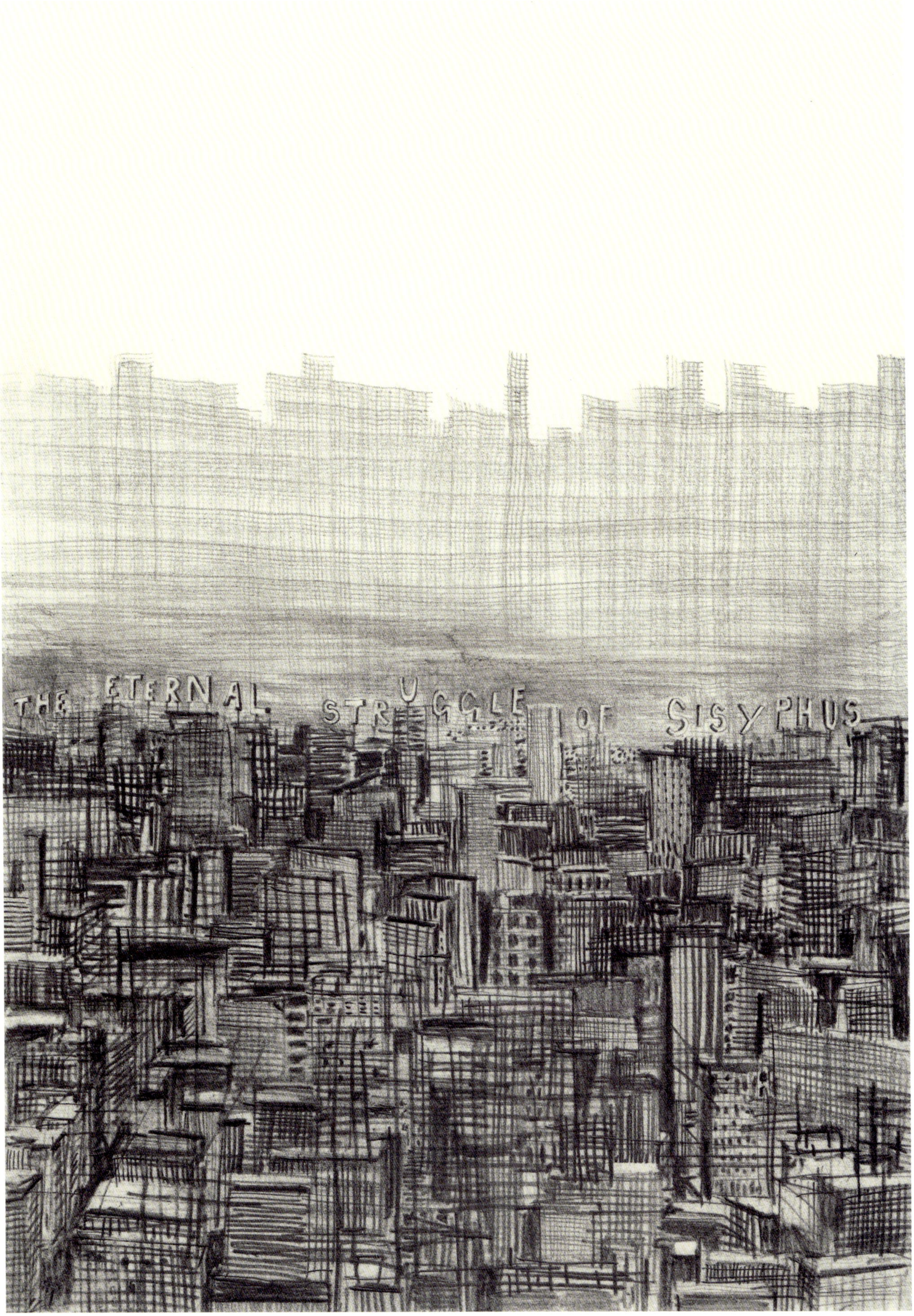

400/2008, 2008

#5/2010 (SEVERAL THOUGHTS), 2010

The Disenchanted Dream of an Urban Poet

Julie Enckell Julliard

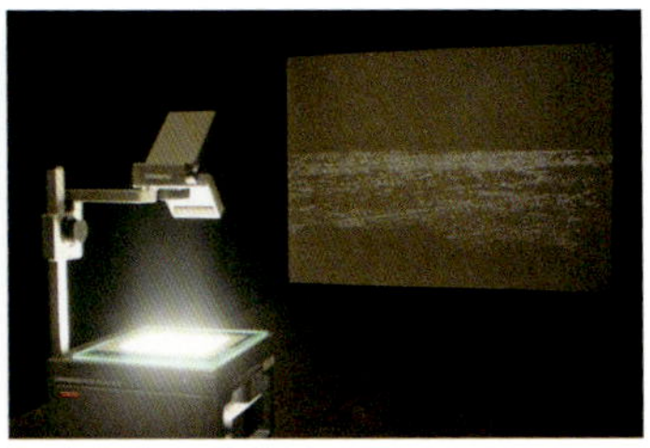

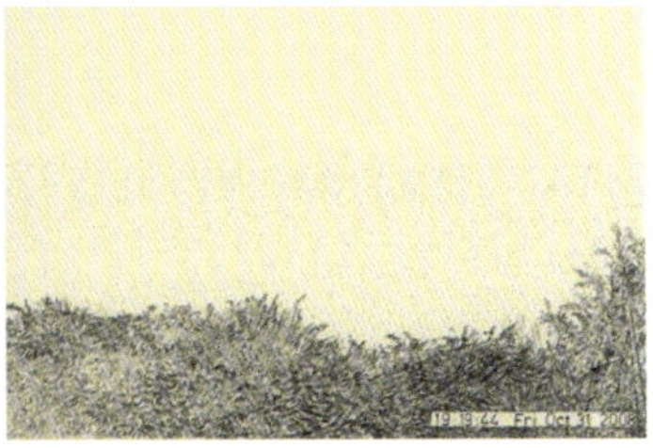

#4, 2008
Drawing on perforated paper, (21.5 × 27.5 cm) framed between two glass plates (32 × 32 cm) on an overhead projector
Collection Musée Jenisch Vevey

One projection, two landscapes. One is drawn, stamped, and mounted on the glass of an overhead projector; it shows a field of wheat scorched by the midday sun. The other, projected onto the wall, offers the vision of a vast urban sprawl by night, with just the lights glowing in the dark to hint at its expanse. Two opposing points of view connecting the microcosm to the macrocosm. An undeniably poetic wellspring is apparent in the magically contrasted combination of the two horizons—one excessively urbanized and plunged in darkness, the other intact, though seared by the projector lamp, embodying the sultry heat of summer. But the meaning of Ante Timmermans' installation cannot be reduced just to this aspect. In confronting the landscapes, the artist also raises a more general question about the passage from a state of nature to a state of culture and how the action of men and the effects of industrialization come to encroach upon expanses of land. This calls to mind the eponymous hero of Italo Calvino's collection of short stories *Marcovaldo, or The Seasons in the City* (1963), whose poetically critical vision underlined the contradictions of urban society as much as its uncanny beauty. In the short story *The Rain and the Leaves*, Marcovaldo, a workman living in a large city in northern Italy, rescues a pot plant from the overly narrow confines of the factory changing rooms and carries it around on the rack of his moped. The hero's daily journeys help the plant to blossom, so that it eventually grows as big as a tree. Another story from the collection, *Moon and GNAC*, recounts how Marcovaldo's children become fascinated with a neon sign for SPAAK-COGNAC, though only the four last letters work properly, and watch it like an unpredictable TV screen as it blinks on and off on the roof opposite their house.

Advertising hoardings, billboards, and slogans displayed across the cityscape play a key role in Ante Timmermans' work. They form a linguistic playing field, ideal for affirming ideas, and offer the city the opportunity literally to "speak": to speak of the system that regulates it, the symbolic violence that its anti-crime rhetoric and need for excessive control inflicts on the daily lives of the inhabitants, and the polysemy of rallying cries that are as sententious as they are untrue. Whether cut short or stripped of context, encrypted or enhanced, the fragments of urban discourse in Timmermans' drawings act as mouthpieces for the system and for the artist himself.

Ante Timmermans is one of those people who hold that technological progress, industrialization, and the rise of mass consumerism—still considered a proof of health and optimism among "hard-working families"—actually feed into a form of poetic disenchantment touched with humor. He prefers the simplicity of pencil and paper to the sophistication of contemporary tools, while his installations use old-fashioned devices such as record players, overhead projectors, and cassette recorders. He argues for a form of impermeability to modernity; the numerous drawings he has produced since the turn of the 21st century deliberately combine sobriety of means and emblems of progress: buildings as far as the eye can see, densely packed, ghostly cities, the peaks of skyscrapers that are as terrifying as they are anonymous. The perspectives are vertiginous, color is rare, and humans are almost entirely absent. Ante Timmermans uses such dehumanized portraits of society to lay claim to a stance as an offbeat observer of the contemporary world. While he lives and works in this context, he cannot find it in himself to identify with it, and therefore has no better choice than to scoff at it.

Ante Timmermans creates his satire of human civilization by constantly switching between urban reality and the imaginary world of childhood. Not only does he use the sorts of stamp every child is familiar with to mark his works, but he also takes the circus as a theme in his drawings. The circus was at the heart of an installation shown at the o.T. Raum für aktuelle Kunst in Lucerne in 2010, which featured a disappointed statement written on the wall itself: ES IST IMMER DIE ALTE LEIER LEIDER (It's always the same old story, sadly). The circus stood for the joyous melancholy of an imaginary place of monotonous entertainment. A "spatialized drawing" in black thread traced the outlines of the circus' rostrum, ladders, and so on, together with a sound loop and projections. A worthy heir to Charlie Chaplin and his film *The Circus,* Ante Timmermans sees the circus as a tragic theater full of measured mechanisms of laughter and dreams, and denounces its lost magic and this means whereby men repress their fellow men. Timmermans also admits to being fascinated by the routine inherent in the circus ring and, similarly, by all closed-circuit processes. Several of his drawings evoke the dullness of daily work and the excesses of bureaucracy, describing a form of monotony contrary to creativity; the emphatic urban constructions that he imagines are called into play to reflect a productivity drive that is incompatible with human functions, with the complexity of toxic architectural structures mirroring the unhealthy, sterile ambitions of industrial civilizations.

Forms of play and entertainment are recurrent in his work and are always seen as a means of expressing a kind of melancholy. Some drawings feature fireworks, washed free of color to resemble weeping willows, to the detriment of the bright hues of the beams of light of which they consist. In another work, a vast neon sign reading PLAYTIME stands ironically on a roundabout overhung by a gallows, echoing the posture of a puppet that has taken the place of a traffic policeman [p. 40]. Does the drawing evoke a child's game or the dissonance of our daily route to work? It is almost impossible not to be reminded of Jacques Tati's 1967 film *Playtime* which paints a portrait of an all-powerful bureaucracy verging on the absurd in the immense modern construction that the hero goes on exploring throughout the film. Like Charlie Chaplin and Marcovaldo, Monsieur Hulot is an offbeat observer of modernity, wittily denouncing its excesses. Ante Timmermans is inspired by the same sources of comedy, revisiting the talent of those predecessors who denounced the excesses of progress by celebrating the inventiveness of the eccentric and the poor. There is one difference, however: Timmermans cultivates a kind of distance, usually managing to avoid featuring in the work himself. Yet despite this, human presence is hinted at everywhere: low-angle shots recall man's puny size in comparison to

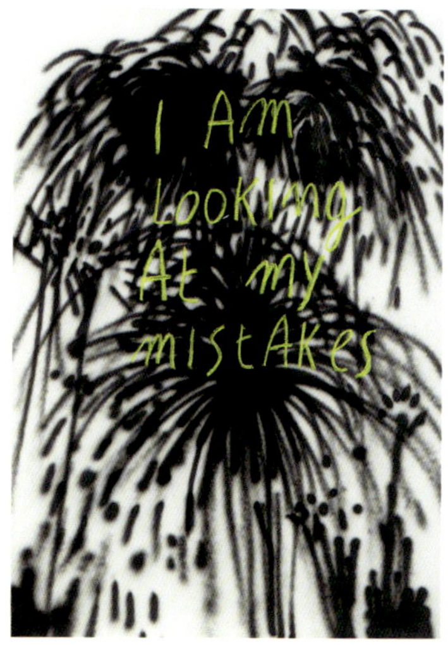

WHATAREYOUDOING? (POESIE DER LANGEWEILE), 2010
Spray paint and oil stick on paper,
180.5 × 119.8 cm
Courtesy Galerie Barbara Seiler, Zurich

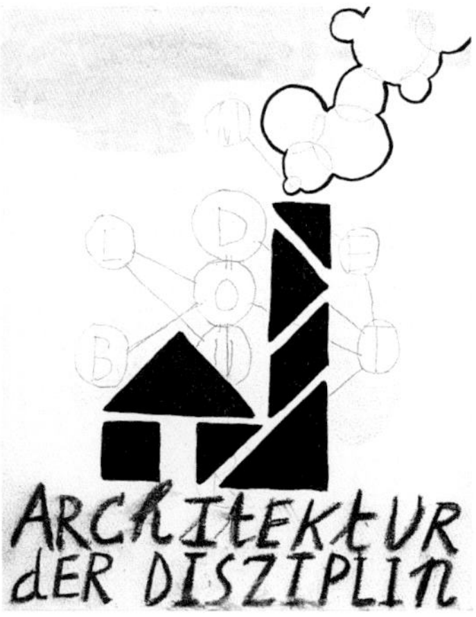

SYSTEME, 2011
Pencil, ink, gouache, and charcoal on canvas, 50 × 40 cm
Courtesy Galerie Barbara Seiler, Zurich

the structures all around him, while viewpoints from overhead, which are in some ways reminiscent of the omniscient gaze of a deity, create the impression that the great architect of the universe is observing the downfall of his creation.

The extreme concision and effectiveness of the composition, often accompanied by comments or puns blending irony and existential questions, lend the drawings the impact of press cartoons. Some viewers will notice analogies with posters for the Situationist International, the protests of May 1968, and, more recently, the banners waved by French trade unionists demonstrating in 2009, when the economic crisis and forced redundancies were at their height. The Situationist movement was among the first critics of urbanity, from the foundation of the Situationist International in 1957 to the publication of Guy Debord's *Society of the Spectacle* in 1967 and Henri Lefebvre's *Production of Space* in 1971. Student protest movements saw the city as the site not only of revolt, but also where their future lives were being decided. Their protests reflect an initial form of occupation of urban space, underpinned by the desire to "change the city to change life."[1] This was the thinking behind *New Babylon*, the utopian project developed by Constant Nieuwenhuys (1920–2005), which is of considerable interest to Ante Timmermans. Nieuwenhuys, who cofounded the Experimentele Groep in Holland with Karel Appel and was the leading theorist behind the CoBrA group, was a member of the Situationist movement from 1958 to 1960 before deciding to reorganize urban space *ab nihilo*. He dreamed of freeing the city from the alienating yoke of productivity and turning it into a space of leisure and creativity. The scale models and drawings he left adumbrate Timmermans' work in their ambition, colored with the ideals of the postwar period that aimed to improve social cohesion through new ways of interconnecting social spaces.

Timmermans' work is powered by a drive to appropriate urban space. However, the playful reactivity inherent in it connects him with other contemporary artists such as David Shrigley or Dan Perjovschi, with his graffiti inscribed on museum walls. Perjovschi's drawings, deeply rooted in the present, are a caustic mirror held up to the world, reflecting the place occupied by the artist. However, Timmermans' work has a poetic dimension above and beyond such preoccupations; its specificity takes him closer to the art of Markus Raetz. Raetz "entered" drawing though the press—his first published drawings were caricatures in a satirical weekly—before discovering a love of words, while developing a playful approach to language. His work was later driven by tender, silent, melancholy poetry, centered on revealed or dual images of the world and of the self.

The motifs that fill Ante Timmermans' compositions are very different from those of Markus Raetz, of course, but the art of words does offer a unique way to translate a feeling of existential isolation or to explore our perception of reality. Timmermans is a moonstruck fool, a *Pierrot lunaire*, who studies the world with a gaze that is both jubilant and disenchanted, recalling its duplicity. Such dual or transformed images are a cornerstone of Raetz's oeuvre, challenging the subjectivity of points of view by creating the illusion of a form of magic that is as virtuoso as it is simple. This is the same tactic used by Timmermans in *#4*, 2008.

1
Philippe Simay, "Une autre ville pour une autre vie. Henri Lefebvre et les Situationnistes," *Métropoles*, vol. 4, 2008, p. 202-213.

Timmermans' close links with German-speaking Switzerland also feeds into a series of ironic drawings on the theme of the identity of the place in which he now lives, Zurich. One drawing presents a ghost city bearing the inscription A.L.P.T.R.A.U.M. ("nightmare" in German), playing on the link between the Alps and the painful imprisonment that they suggest. Another drawing bears the word S**WITZ**ERLAND ("Witz" means "joke"), as if the country's name itself contained a trick of identity. Such considerations also extend to his native Belgium, where the piles of animal feed protected by plastic sheeting weighed down by tyres scattered along the roadsides are ironically identified as "Flemish monuments" (*#9/2010 (Flämisches Denkmal)*, 2010).

Underlying Timmermans' pictorial narratives is a deeper question about his own self. Several urban visions can be read as portraits of the artist. Such are his "Mind Maps," which denounce both omnipresent social controls on individuals and the limits we all impose on ourselves: the measured mechanism of the social system echoes that of our own mental structure. *#5/2010 (Several Thoughts)* features thoughts translated as a series of lines, strangely reminiscent of the ordinary pattern of skyscrapers. And when the artist claims "Ich bin auch eine Zeichnung" (I am a drawing too), he maintains the impersonal typography of road signs, using the drawing as the site for a quest for identity. By what means do we perceive reality? Are the images generated by the artist a truthful reflection of it? By focusing his attention on the social system and its excesses, the artist raises the vital question of how humans function and where their limits lie, laying the responsibility for its current failings squarely at their feet.

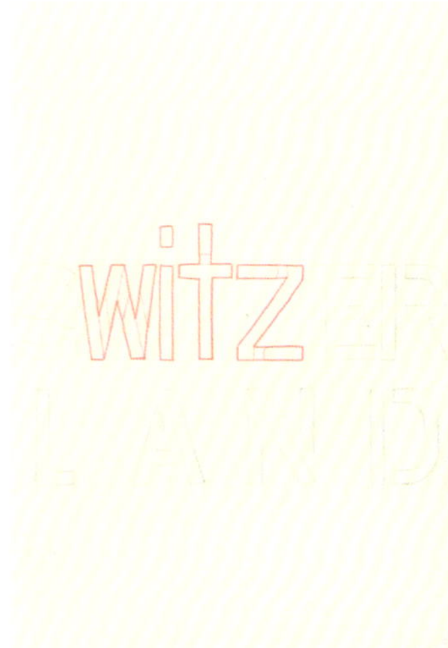

393/2008, 2008
Pencil and colored pencil on paper, 21.2 × 14.5 cm
Private collection, Belgium

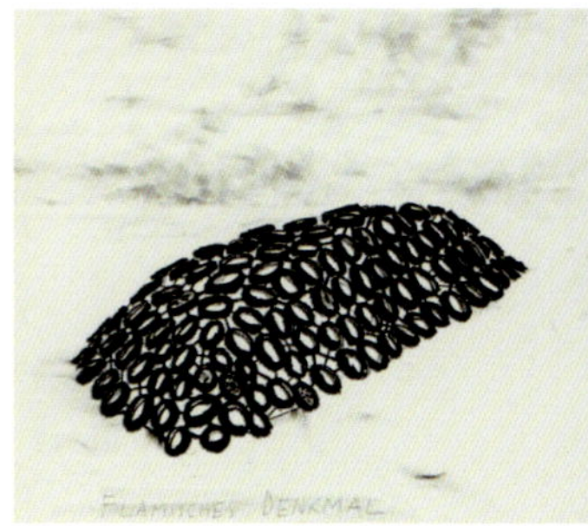

#9/2010 (FLÄMISCHES DENKMAL), 2010
Pencil and oil pastel on paper, 65 × 75 cm
Private collection, Belgium

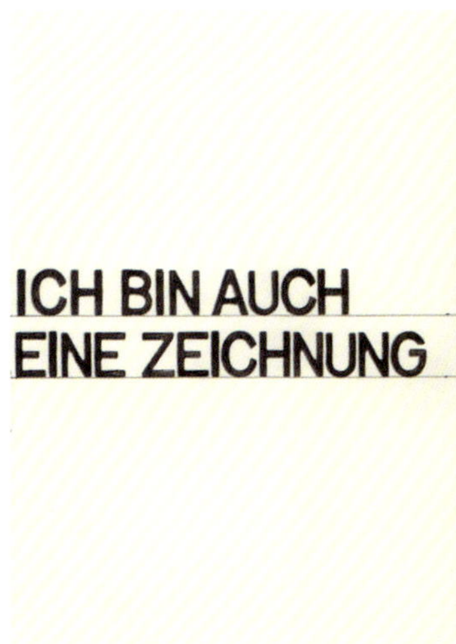

465/2009, 2009
Pencil on paper, 21.2 × 14.5 cm
Private collection

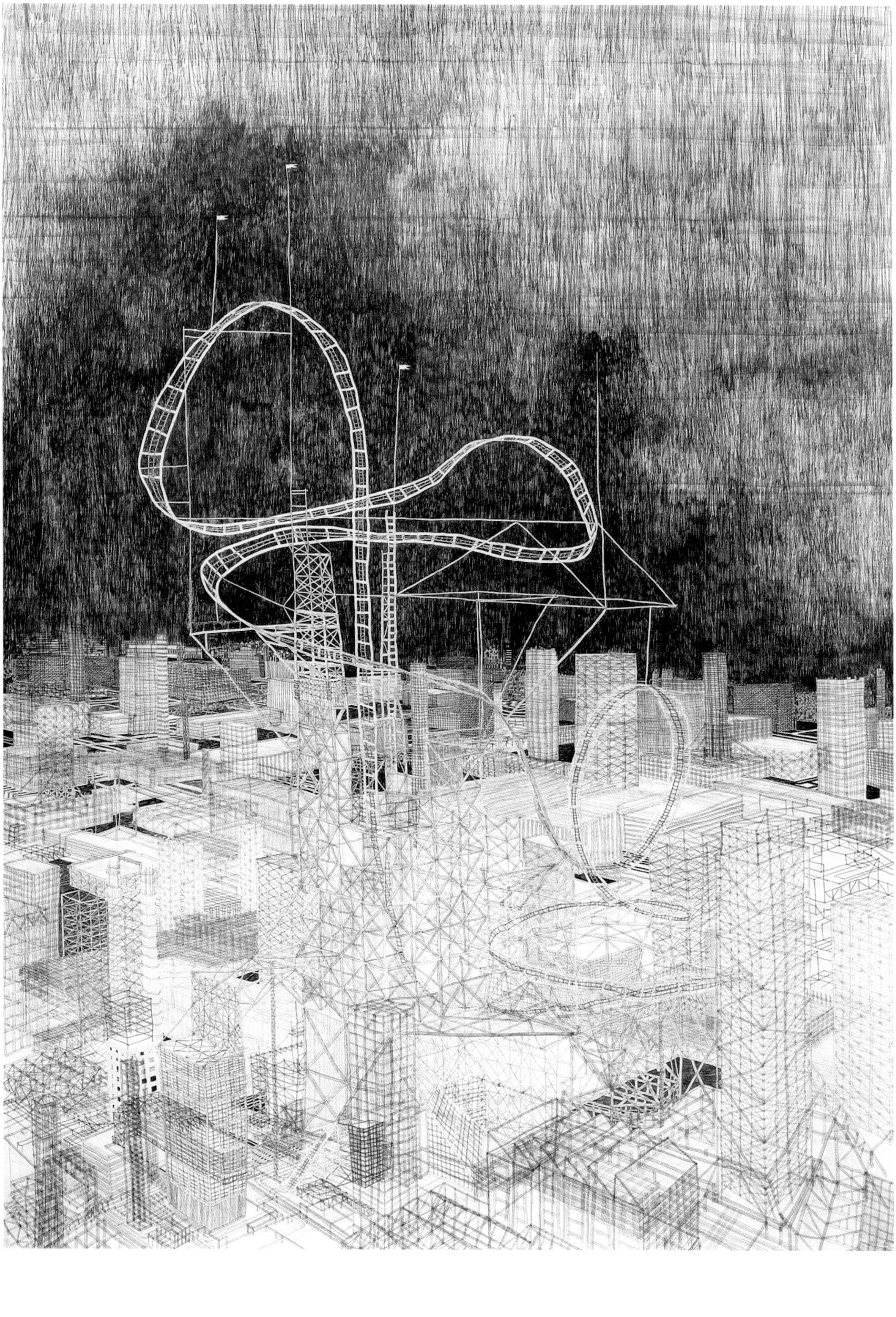

#2/2010 (FABRICATION), 2010

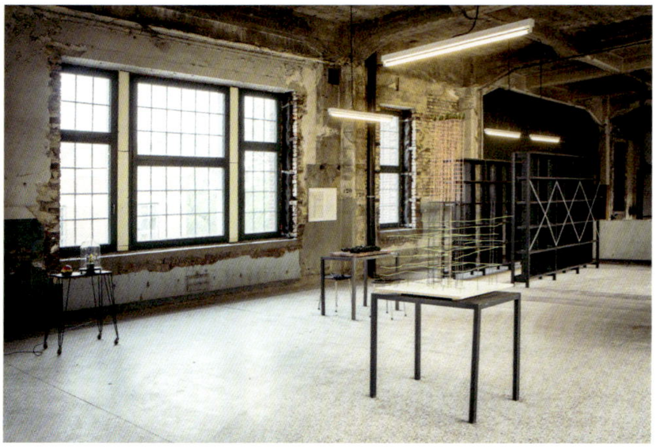

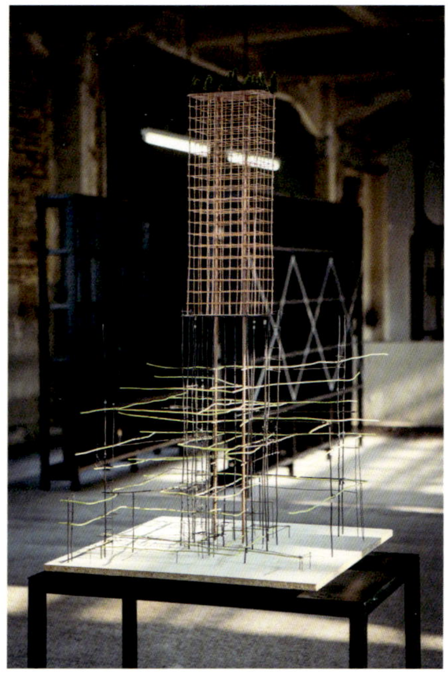

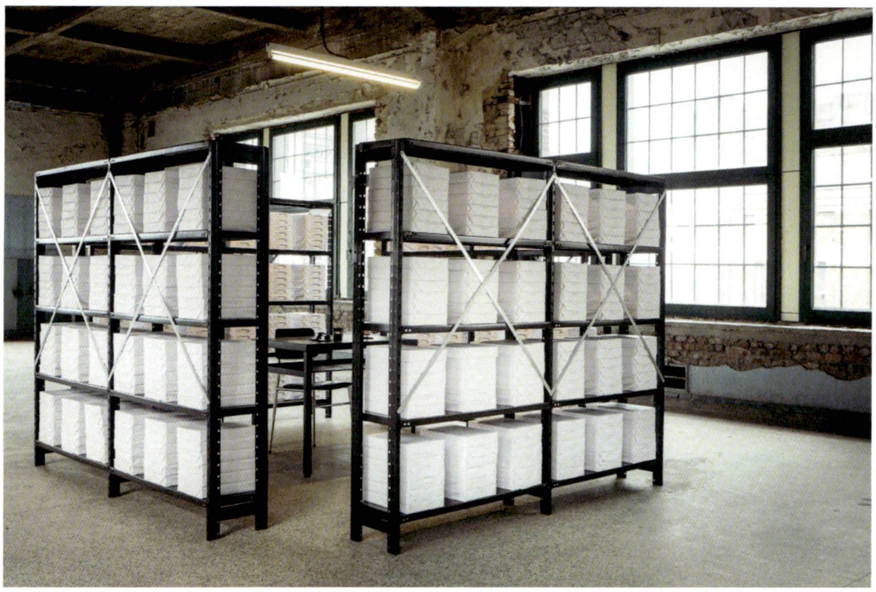

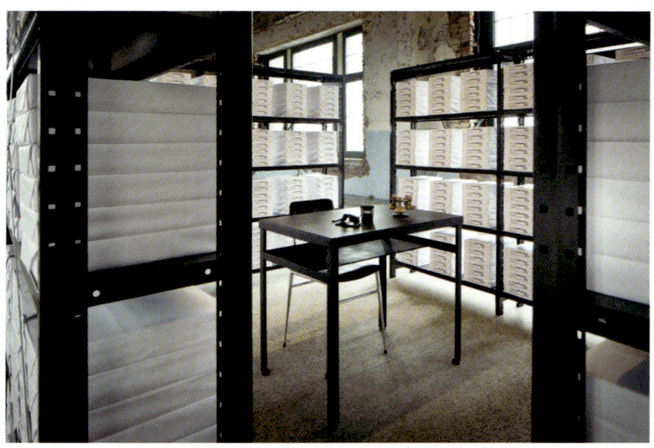

Showing and Drawing Thinking …
Ante Timmermans in Conversation with Konrad Bitterli*

KONRAD BITTERLI We've already had various conversations about your artistic work, including in the context of your 2010 exhibition at the Galerie Barbara Seiler. You came to the fore particularly on account of your graphic work. I'd like to approach our conversation from a different angle, arrive at your work through the back door to a certain extent. Presumably it would be very little known that at the very beginning of the 2000s you were already doing what are known as spatial drawings?

ANTE TIMMERMANS Right from the start I've been interested in developing the content of my work. It has always arisen from a thought process where I've imposed no boundaries on myself regarding medium or material. The "decision" in favor of drawing as a medium was made very spontaneously, and almost of necessity. For me it was and is the direct link between thinking and visualizing (drawing), it's like writing, without getting deflected by a working process. People think and write what they think, I think and draw what I think. At the same time the medium offers the opportunity to bring a new "world of thoughts" into being, using simple "cheap" materials—pencils and paper. The drawings are associative links between thoughts, very spatial. I still remember, to start with they were small spatial "exercises" or discoveries close to my worktable in the studio. Then very soon I made a first large spatial drawing *in situ*. So big that visitors could not only walk through the drawing, but in fact they really had to in order to discover the different details—zooming in and out physically. You could look at the drawing from different—individual—perspectives. From that moment on the question "what is a drawing?" has fascinated me. Projected drawings, video fragments, installative drawings, and so on came along later.

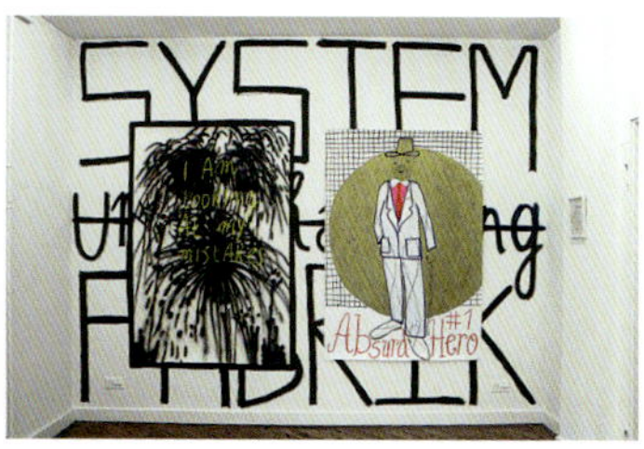

POESIE DER LANGEWEILE, exhibition view, Galerie Barbara Seiler, Zurich, 2010

The search for a drawing in space, the directness, the fragility, the simultaneous process of thinking and working was a very thrilling challenge, and still is. Afterward, with this experience—the specific conditions of a spatial drawing—it was just as interesting to draw on paper again.

KONRAD BITTERLI I'd like to go into the relationship of the drawing to space you're talking about a little more deeply. The installation as a drawing in space, but also the spatial aspect of the drawing itself. How do you see the relationship of installation to drawing? Is the latter something like a preliminary study for spatial works, or are they independent strands of work? Or to put it the other way round: to what extent has drawing changed as a result of your experience with space?

ANTE TIMMERMANS My drawings do in fact often have a powerful spatial effect. Sometimes I've been asked, "When will you implement this drawing?"; the answer is "Never"—the fact that it is already possible to imagine it—just with pencil on paper, wonderful!—has always been enough for me.

When I started making spatial drawings, for me it was certainly not a transposition of an earlier drawing. Each work functions autonomously. Spatial drawing and drawing stand alongside one another and influence (feed into) one another. I have never made a preliminary study.
A preliminary study would mean that I plan the work and don't permit any mistakes or surprises to disturb my thought process or the development of the work (action–reaction), and so I'd lose the directness and fragility. Every work, every presentation is an attempt to visualize my thoughts. Of course symbols or elements from my drawings sometimes recur in a spatial drawing. A new meaning and further thoughts then arise from this confrontation.

The movement from spatial drawing to drawing on paper is very interesting. For instance, if I attach a taut string to another string, then I need a third string to make the first taut string straight again—somehow it sound very technical and theoretical, but actually it's absurd and very interesting to draw on paper again with this thought in mind. In my large drawings the idea of "zooming in and out" has had a great influence—the impossibility of taking everything in at one glance, and the possibility of losing yourself in the various details.

KONRAD BITTERLI You speak of "zooming in and out." That applies in equal measure to your presentations of drawings which are often arranged spatially, here I'm thinking of your exhibition in the Croxhapox in Ghent (2005), for example, where you laid drawings out on tables, thereby to a certain extent placing them in the space. Does that become even clearer in later large-scale presentations?

ANTE TIMMERMANS Exactly. I took this idea of "zooming in and out" further in installative presentations. For me each presentation is an instantaneous snapshot, with various works (drawings, spatial drawings, projections, etc.) coming together—thus different connections come about and new thoughts are generated. A presentation imposing its presence functions for me as a "mind-map." The visitor is surrounded by my work, my thoughts. I expect a lot of the viewer, visually and mentally, and hope to trigger a thought process in them too. I use various materials, media, and formats; I use them to play on the expectations and concentration of onlookers. The performative installations are a new development.

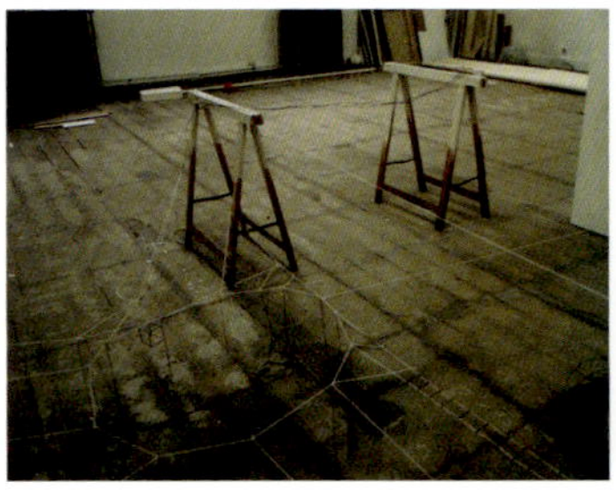

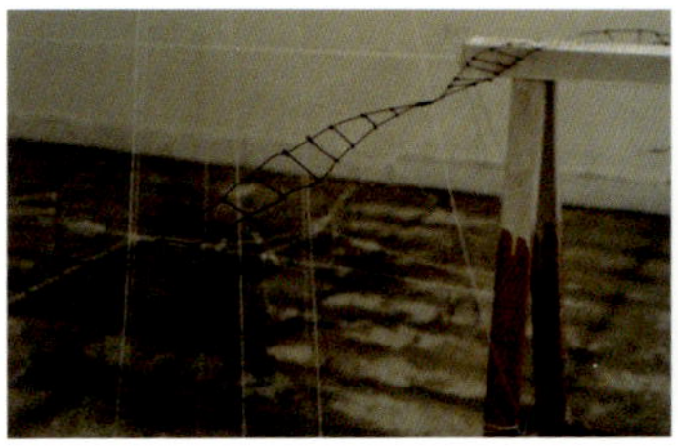

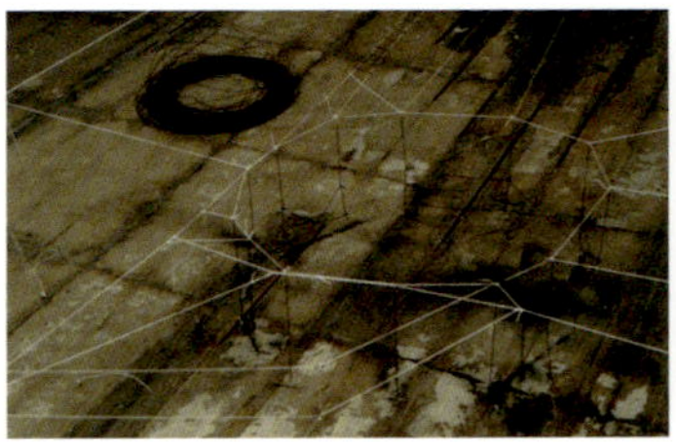

Studio views, Brussels, 2000

KONRAD BITTERLI Let me spend a bit longer on the "spatial drawings": after a longish interruption, in 2010 you once again started creating several such installations in short succession, starting with the one at the o.T. Raum für aktuelle Kunst in Lucerne. Why did you go back to installation after a phase of drawing, and how has the way you deal with space changed since the first spatial drawing? And how have the performative installations developed out of them?

ANTE TIMMERMANS Actually that's not quite correct. In this period, from the first spatial drawing in 2001 until 2010, I carried on exploring the medium of drawing, with spatial drawings, projections, wall drawings, video fragments, etc., and spatial presentations too. They weren't still the same spatial drawings with thread or string, you're right there. It was always a way of going on searching to find out how to deal with my work in a space.

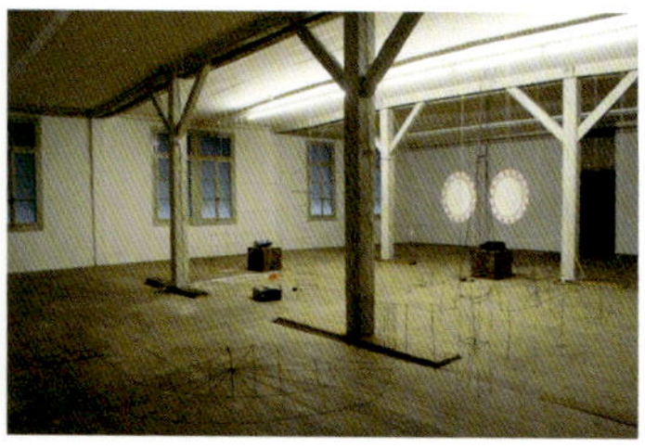

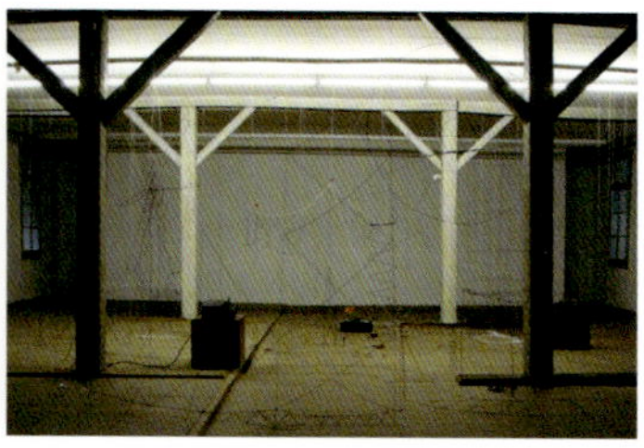

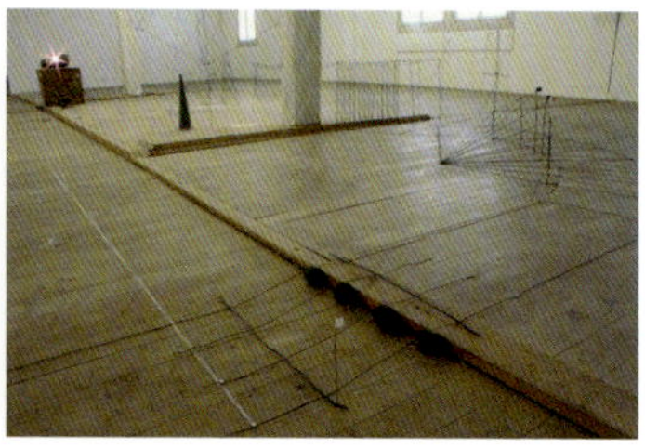

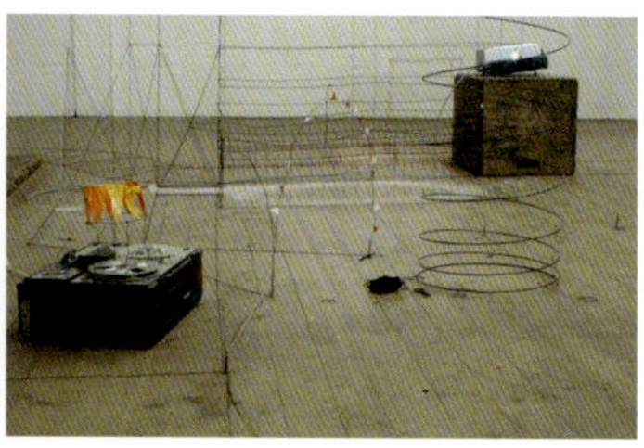

POESIE DES ALLTÄGLICHEN, installation view at o.T. Raum für aktuelle Kunst, Lucerne, 2010

The decision regarding what form the presentation takes is very tied up with the space. For example, at o.T. Raum it was clear to me from the start that I didn't want to build any extra walls, in order to preserve the character of the space. I wanted to play with the space in a very open way. The decision in favor of a "spatial drawing" came about very logically. I also had the possibility of being able to build on site for two to three weeks, which unfortunately one can seldom do in an art world in which speed is called for.

In Barbara Seiler's gallery I then had the opportunity to develop this further visually, and in terms of content. The performative installations developed out of this. For me they are clearly not performances as such. It has to do with an action, so I myself am only a moving object in the installation.

KONRAD BITTERLI At o.T. Raum you wanted to play with the space in an open way. That openness already resonates in the concept of "spatial drawing." At the same time the effect is surprisingly light and fragile, and above all it is characterized by a surprising attention to detail, and is reminiscent of a model, a view of a model landscape.

ANTE TIMMERMANS I've always looked for fragility, lightness, directness—you could also say I've looked for "drawing"—in a variety of media. I've looked for this direct connection between thinking and visualizing, to begin with only with drawing—that was a logical decision—and later with other media too. This direct way of working implies fragility. I didn't want technical questions to put a brake on me.

As for the surprising attention to detail you talk about, I myself don't immediately think of model making. On the one hand I find this idea of "zooming in and out" very exciting, and thus I play with the viewer's concentration—people take a look and go on looking because otherwise they have the feeling that they're missing something. On the other hand this game provokes or confuses viewers by using different scales—which again stimulates the thinking process.

KONRAD BITTERLI In the installation just mentioned, people will be constantly zooming in and out between the overall view and the detail, to use your term. For example, there are miniature garden fences with small red and white flags and cheerful garlands that seem to flutter in the wind. Beside them there's a roundabout that turns on a reel-to-reel tape recorder. A giant wheel is poised over the whole thing, but with a diameter of a little over a meter, the wheel appears tiny in comparison with its real "comrades." They are playful elements. Is your world a happy, light-hearted one?

ANTE TIMMERMANS My world isn't that light-hearted. It tends to be thoughtful, and my thoughts tend to be critical and doubtful. My studio involves a critical coming to terms with everyday things, with the absurdity of life, with boredom. It's about an existence defined by routine. As well as a critical attitude, poetry and humor are very important to me for dealing with it.

When I speak about boredom (for example), I don't mean Sunday afternoon boredom, which is circumstantial boredom. For me it's a matter of a profound, intense boredom, an existential boredom. In our history, and still even today, people have always tried to make things "pleasanter, easier" for human beings. One example is the automation of our work output, which is perhaps not a bad thing in itself. But at the same we have more and more free time. Free time that human beings can no longer fill properly on their own. It's a problem of our modern times. Something that is observable, for instance, in more and more specious solutions and the ever larger entertainment industry. In the end I think that technology hasn't changed things that much for humankind. It's a circular movement, not a linear one. I like to refer to a photograph I took in 1999. This picture immediately inspired and activated my thinking/working process. It's a picture of a neighbor's daily routine. More than ten years later, I increasingly realize how important this picture is for me and for my work. Many elements of my work are present in this picture: the everyday, routine, circling, boredom, drawing (traces), absurdity, humor, poetry.

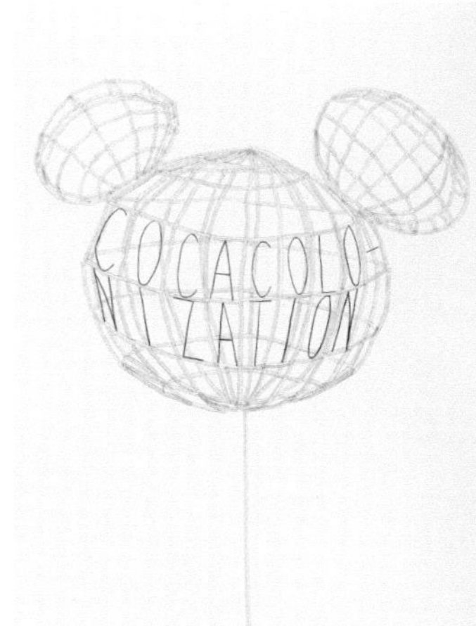

#26/2009 (UNTITLED), 2009
Pencil and chalk on paperboard,
130 × 100 cm
Courtesy Galerie Zink, Berlin

KONRAD BITTERLI This photograph seems to be programmatic for your work. You gave your exhibition at the o. T. the title *Poesie des alltäglichen* (Poetry of Everyday Life). That same year you opened the exhibition *Poesie der Langeweile* (Poetry of Boredom) at Galerie Barbara Seiler. It seems as if the content of your titles is also a program for a society that is going in circles. I remember a text that you projected at the Lucerne exhibition: ES IST IMMER DIE ALTE LEIER LEIDER (It's always the same old story, sadly). At the same time you're "playing" with the endless temptations of our society, and you use the term "Disneyfication" to describe them.

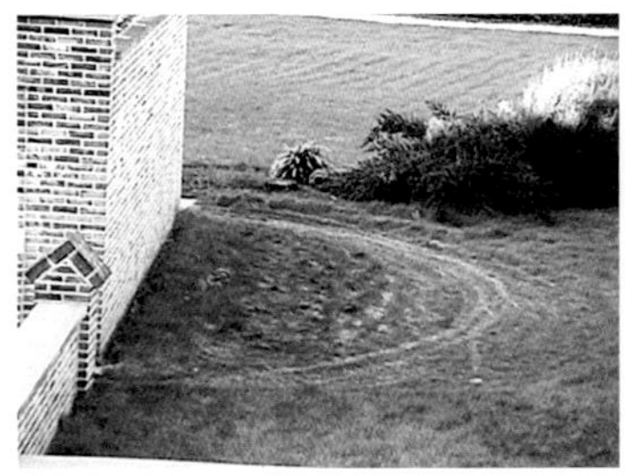
DOKUMENT#1 (SPUREN), 1999
Black and white photograph
Collection of the artist

ANTE TIMMERMANS "Disneyfication," "McDonaldization," "Cocacolonization," are expressions used to denounce the way modern society is developing. A society in which consumption, selling, advertising, and so on, become ever more important, a more and more homogenized, globalized, and perhaps superficial society. It's clearly intended negatively, and our surroundings often also seem as fake as those Disney theme parks. For me that too is a consequence of existential boredom. The entertainment industry tries to fill "the vacuum" in some way. We live in a "fictiory," between fict, fact, fiction, factory, fictitious, and factitious. We aren't experiencing time, we're passing time.

I've been considering these themes for many years. Among the things I'm very fascinated by are the ideas expressed in Constant Nieuwenhuys' *New Babylon*. I've drawn a great many towns, villages, city-maps, landscapes. They were always developing, in the process, but EMPTY. There was ever less room for people, for humankind. All that was left there were the traces of thoughts and actions by human beings. For days, sometimes months, on end, I was busy constructing emptiness in a drawing, like a monotonous, routine artist/worker.

Because I was a little afraid of becoming an artist going round in circles myself, in 2010 I very deliberately chose the titles *Poesie des alltäglichen* and *Poesie der Langeweile*. I wanted to show poetry, humor, absurdity more in my work again. It was important for me, for myself. The theme has remained unchanged. It's still the same old story, sadly.

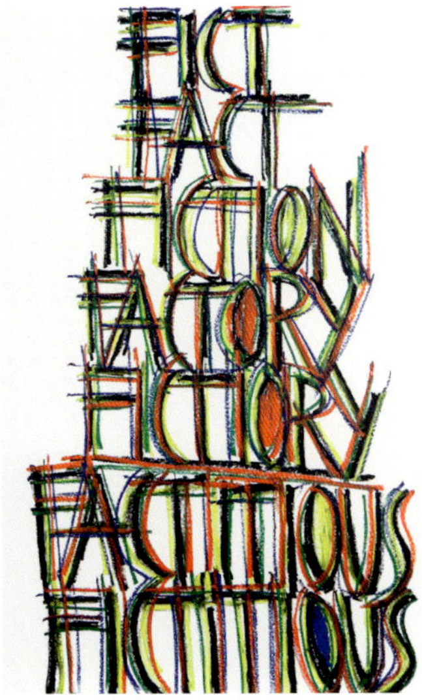

FICT-FACT, 2011
Oil stick on paper, 180 × 120 cm
·Courtesy Galerie Zink, Berlin

KONRAD BITTERLI Our conversation is also destined to go round in a circle in the same way: you speak of routine, a daunting concept for anyone creating art. This makes me think of your early small-format drawings which remind me of diary-type notes—and therefore of routine. In them we come across railway tracks, circus tents, poles erected at fairs, covered haystacks, pylons, details of landscapes, animals, but never people.

ANTE TIMMERMANS I find the concept of "diary-type notes" totally inappropriate in connection with my small-format drawings. For me a "diary" is something private, written daily and chronologically, which I can't connect with those drawings in any way.

In 2001 I finished my art studies at Sint-Lukas in Brussels, and after that I worked full-time for a few years—from 9 to 5—as well as trying to make progress as an artist. At that time I was commuting almost every day between my flat and my workplace. These drawings were produced in that situation—before work, after work, on the train, in the car, in traffic jams or in my little attic studio. I still remember how I took an empty reading book—with just blank pages—and on the first page wrote: "—Beeld als oorsprong-juni 2002—... " ("Picture as origin—June 2002 ..."). I believe that before thoughts can be formulated, before they can be put into words and spoken, they are pictures in one's head. I wanted to visualize those pictures to show and draw thinking. Many of these drawings were made while I myself was moving, or after. I've also described them as "observations in the past." They are visual memories that arrive on paper through a process of observing, thinking and drawing.

I still do those little drawings, influenced by my observations—in the widest sense of the word. It seems to be a never-ending process. After ten years all these little drawings are the backbone of my oeuvre, or as you yourself once said: the letters, the alphabet of my work.

KONRAD BITTERLI Picture as origin—I find that completely apt. With the small-format drawings you've developed a vocabulary that you refer to for your large-format drawings. It seems to me as if the motifs in the latter are being overlaid and becoming denser. When did the large formats start, and what prompted the change of format, or what impact has it had on your creative work?

ANTE TIMMERMANS It isn't that simple to answer that question, because many things come about or happen spontaneously in the studio. The first large-format drawings were done in 2006, perhaps from a need to draw on a bigger scale and more physically, to feel movement more myself, circling, for example *Routinefication* (2006). Sometimes I then spent weeks or months drawing, and routine, boredom, control were not only the content, but part of the working process too, like *Bored Control* (2006) for instance. Drawings like *Cityscape* (2006), for example, refer to the spatial drawings. Or sometimes it was simply a feeling that I should use a large format for a particular drawing.

A lot more is going on visually in the big drawings, logically somehow. At that time I had enlarged my format, but I didn't want to adapt my drawing materials. Large-format drawings generally involve a longer working period, therefore several thoughts coincide. It is even more a process of thinking, acting, and reacting to what is happening, including unexpected things that happen on the paper. What in the case of small drawings really develops in a series, happens on one sheet of paper in the case of large-format drawings.

For my last big drawings, such as the *Poesie der Langeweile* series (2010), I wanted to work in the same way as with the small drawings. Therefore I adapted the format of my large drawings, and used the same proportional relationship of the paper that the small A5 drawings have. Which was actually a very logical decision, as well as being the right one.

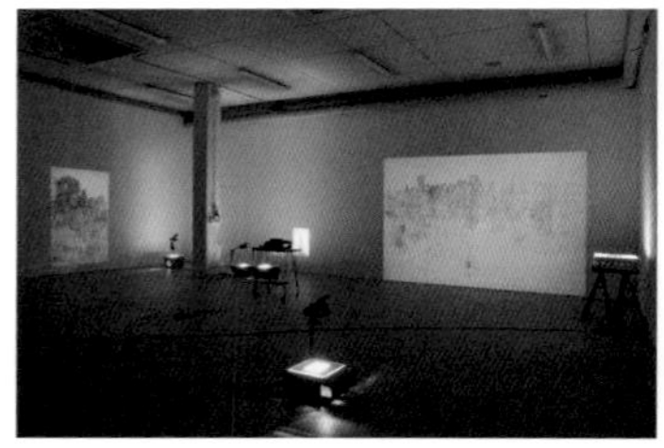

BARRACK–MAPPING THE CITY (Proposal#1), installation view at HISK, Antwerp, 2006

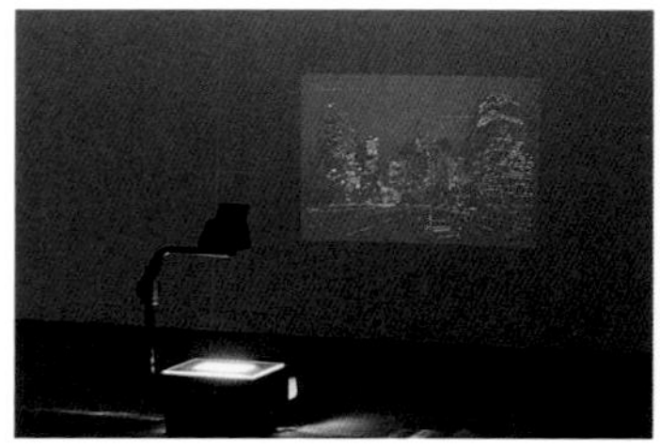

#2, 2006
Drawing on perforated paper (21.5 X 27.5 cm), framed between 2 glass plates (32 × 32 cm) on an overhead projector
Collection Nedko Solakov

KONRAD BITTERLI To a certain extent small and large formats coincide in one group of works. I am thinking of your projection drawings in which you put a traditional pencil drawing on paper, but at the same time perforate it and project it on to the wall via an overhead projector. That's a surprising contribution to the theme of drawing, which is illuminated as it were. An extremely complex shift from small to large format is revealed in those, in one case from a landscape drawing virtually looking like an Old Master in detail, to an overhead view of a mega-city at night. How did you arrive at this unusual format/medium? And what are you aiming at with the simultaneity of two graphic traditions, or two pictorial concepts?

ANTE TIMMERMANS That's a very interesting comment, because different things are happening precisely with that work. At that time I was interested in these “empty landscapes,” but also fascinated by how, for instance, a functional factory landscape or a gray city landscape suddenly looks so beautiful and poetic at night. I wanted to narrate this thought. At the same time it was a further examination of the theme of drawing, and as I've already said, unexpected things sometimes happen in the studio. When I'd laid my first perforated drawing down on the overhead projector —and then this large projection—it was a surprising effect for me, visually, but also in terms of content. Sometimes—very rarely—key works come about in this way in my working process. Works in which different elements, different thoughts coincide in the right way.

The projection work you talk of does indeed show a projection of a sprawling mega-city at night, and on the projector there is an old, yellowing paper with a landscape drawing in pencil. Again there is no figure viewed from behind, but in spite of that it is reminiscent of Caspar David Friedrich. Although this work actually shows the opposite of Romanticism. It expresses admiration for the poetry of urbanization and industrialization. But anyone who looks closer will see a report of the date and time at the bottom right of the drawing, a reference to a city cam or CCTV camera. A less romantic detail.

KONRAD BITTERLI In your most recent works the performative aspect has become increasingly important. You speak of performative installations. I'd like to finish off by venturing to take a peek at the work you have exhibited at *Manifesta 9* which also contains performative elements, doesn't it?

ANTE TIMMERMANS The work I developed for *Manifesta 9* is called *Make a Molehill Out of a Mountain (of Work)*. Among other things it shows the absurdity and mental claustrophobia of our bureaucracy.

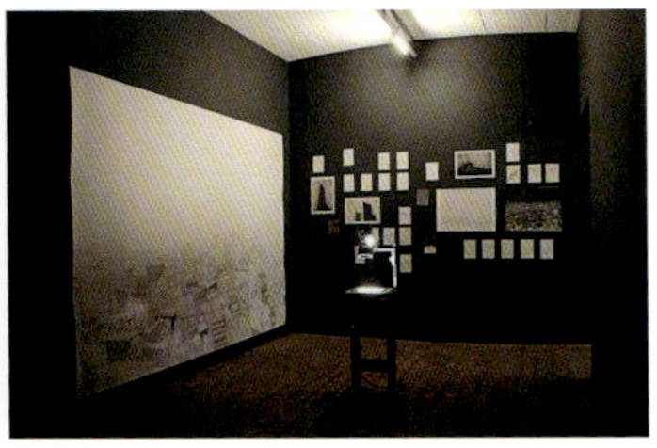

Ariane de Rothschild Prize, MINDSCAPE#2, Installation view at Tour & Taxis, Brussels, 2008

The central part of this work is a performative installation. By that I mean that it isn't really a performance, but a total installation for which I require action. Afterward the installation shows the traces of my action. Really I am then only a moving object in my installation. Movement, action has always been inherent to my subject matter: circling, routine, drawing, traces, and so on. One of my first works (1999) arose from a circular movement in a space with another person. For seven minutes, seven steps forward and seven steps back, with a metronome in the middle to dictate the rhythm of the movement. Afterward I noticed that we'd made a circular drawing (tracks) in the dust. At the time I called it "ennui contrôlé" (controled boredom).

I'm not concerned only with action. With these new performative works I place myself among the public. Recently I increasingly seek discourse, confrontation, conversation—social contact, as a supplementary part of my artistic activity. Things always go in phases with me. And I think, after all the talking, I'll soon need to be alone again—a period of thinking in the studio.

*This interview was conducted by email between December 2011 and February 2012.

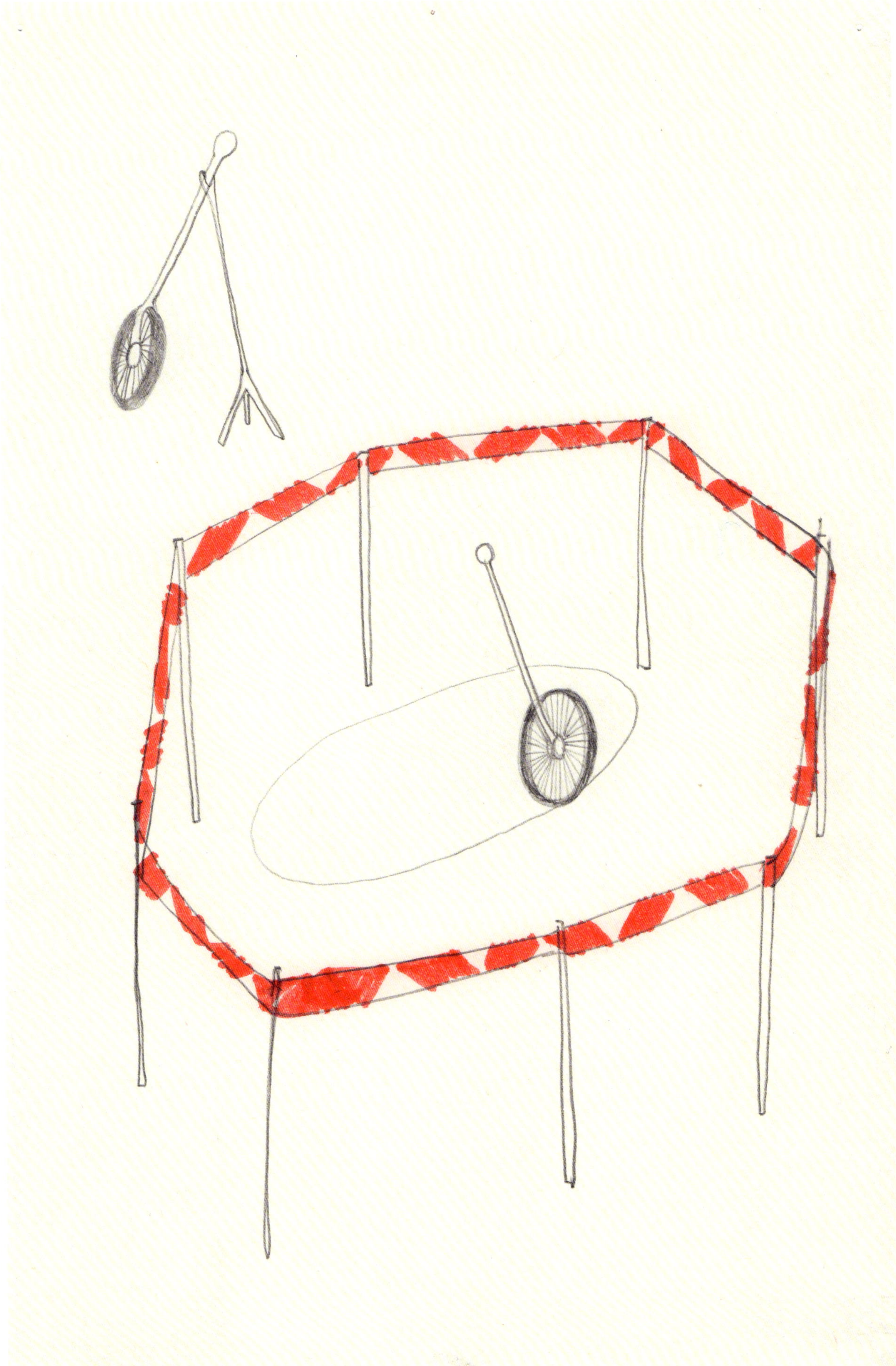

58/2002, 2002

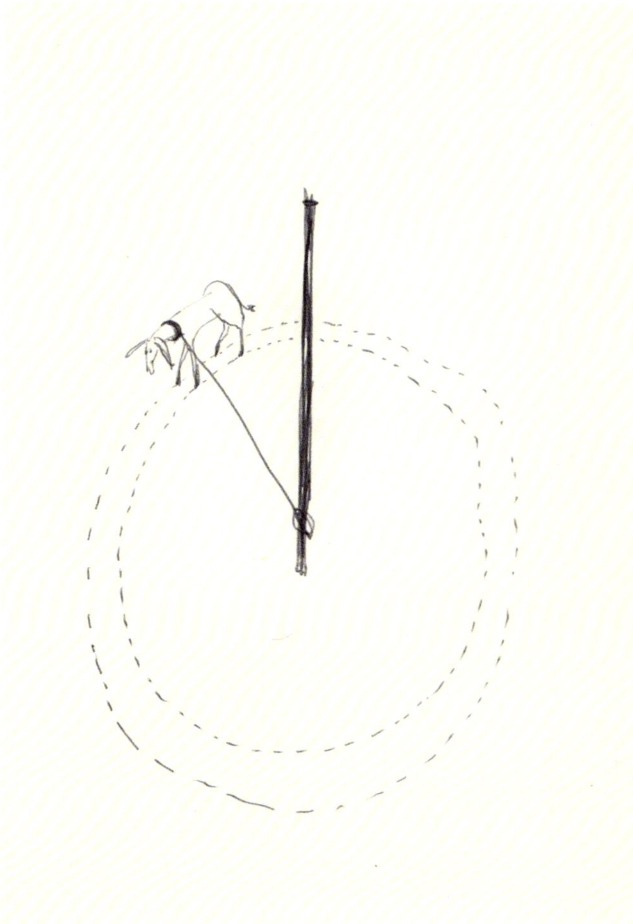

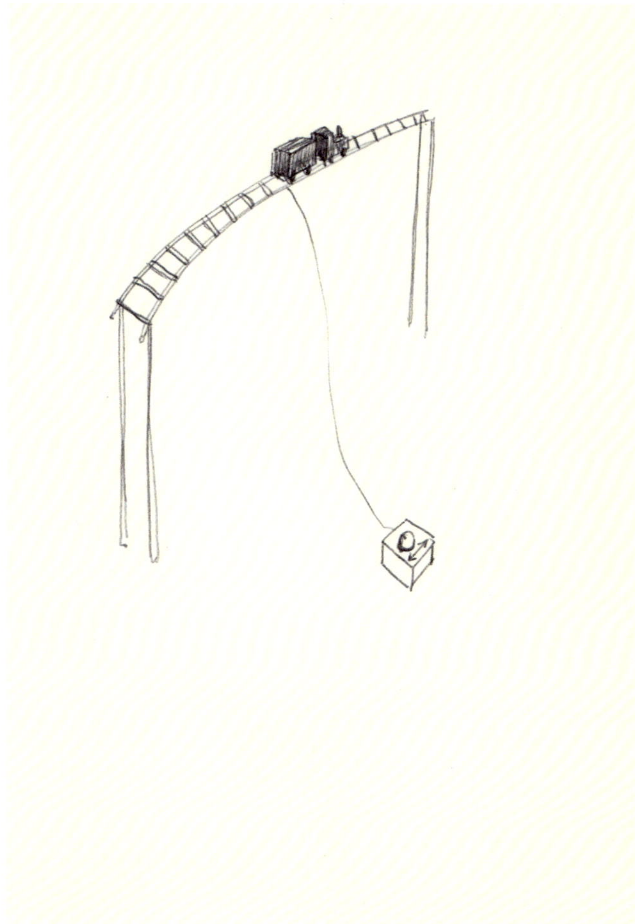

19/2002, 2002
9/2002, 2002

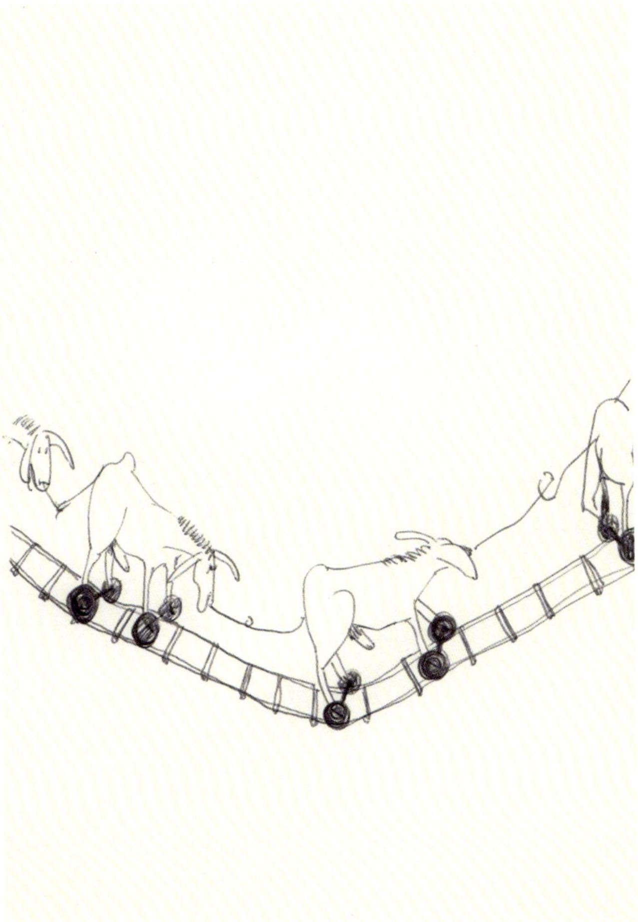

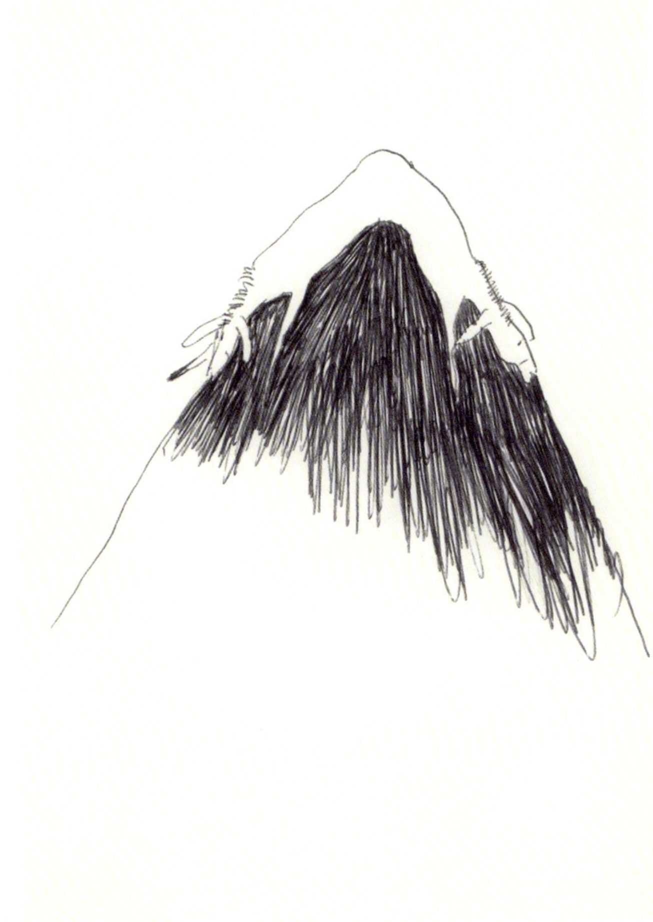

20/2002, 2002
22/2002, 2002

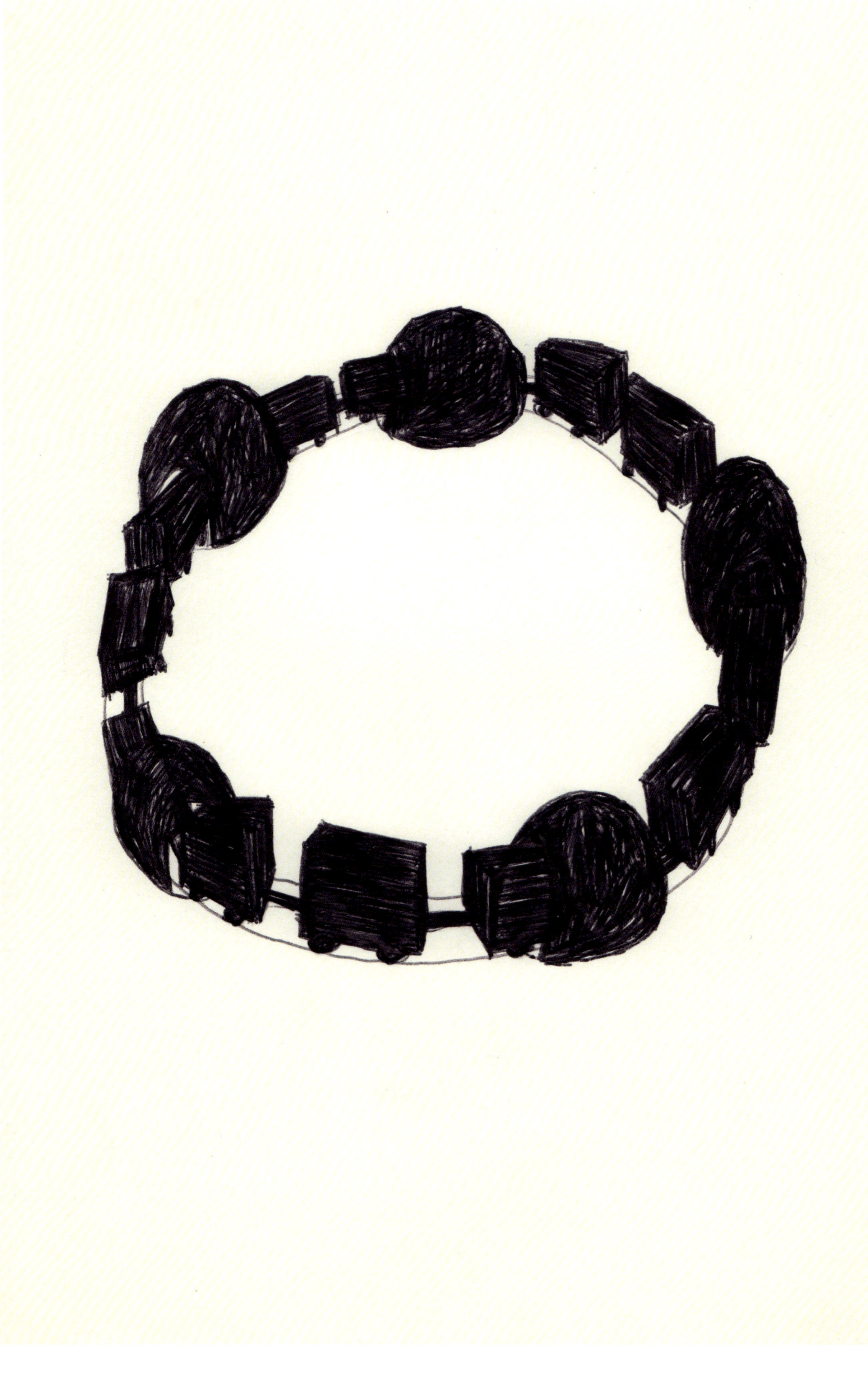

132/2003, 2003

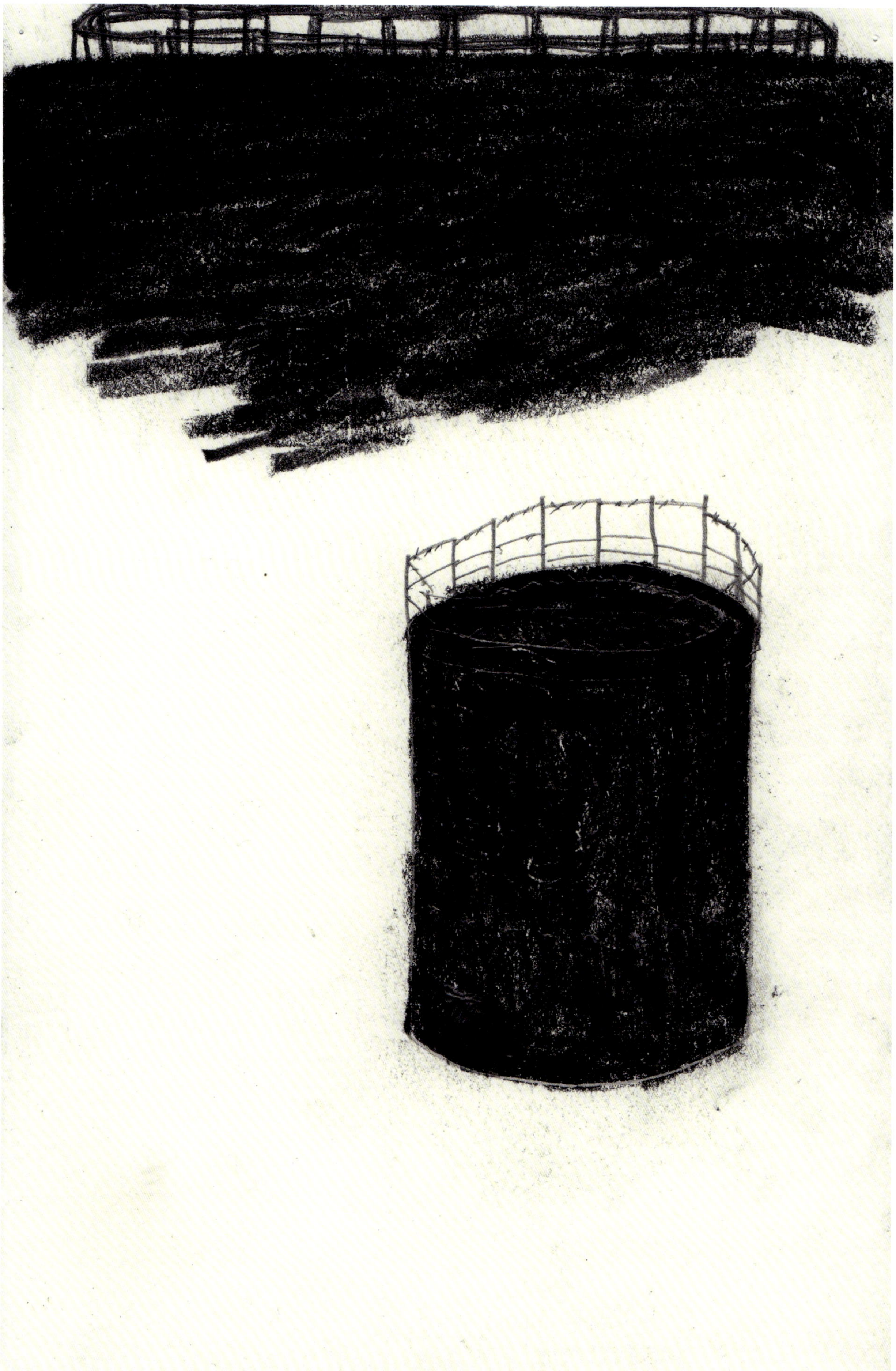

163/2003, 2003

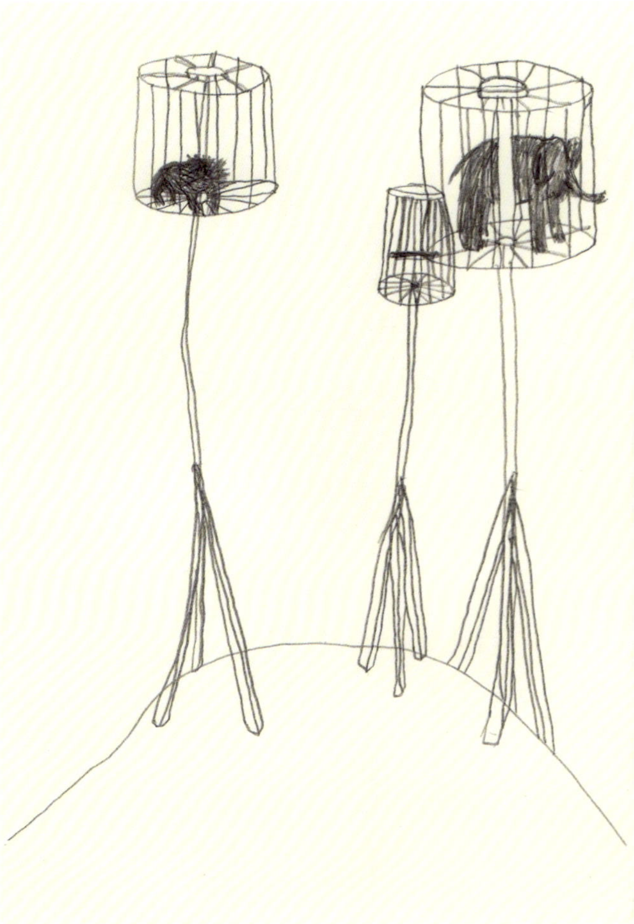

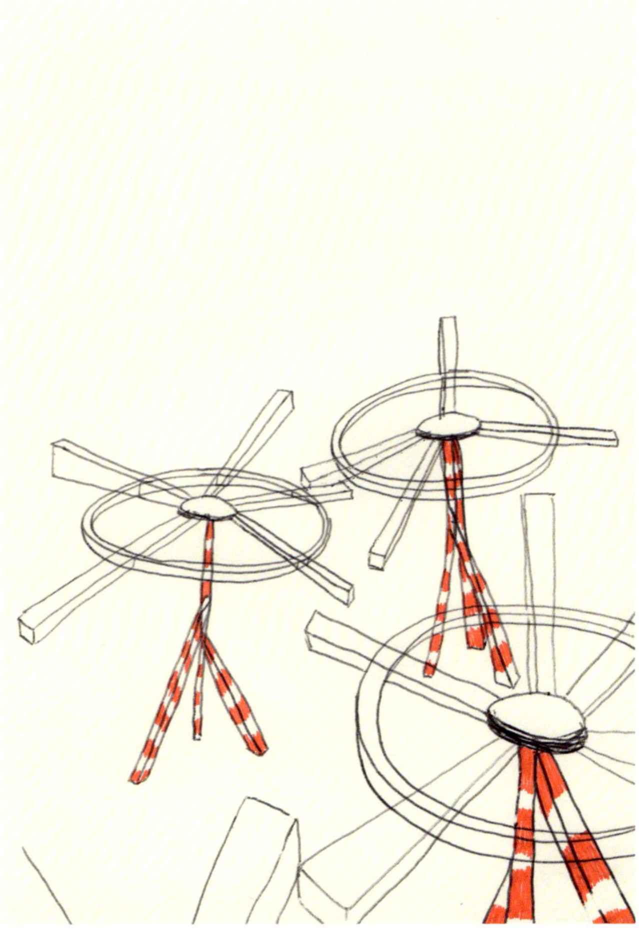

176/2003, 2003
186/2003, 2003

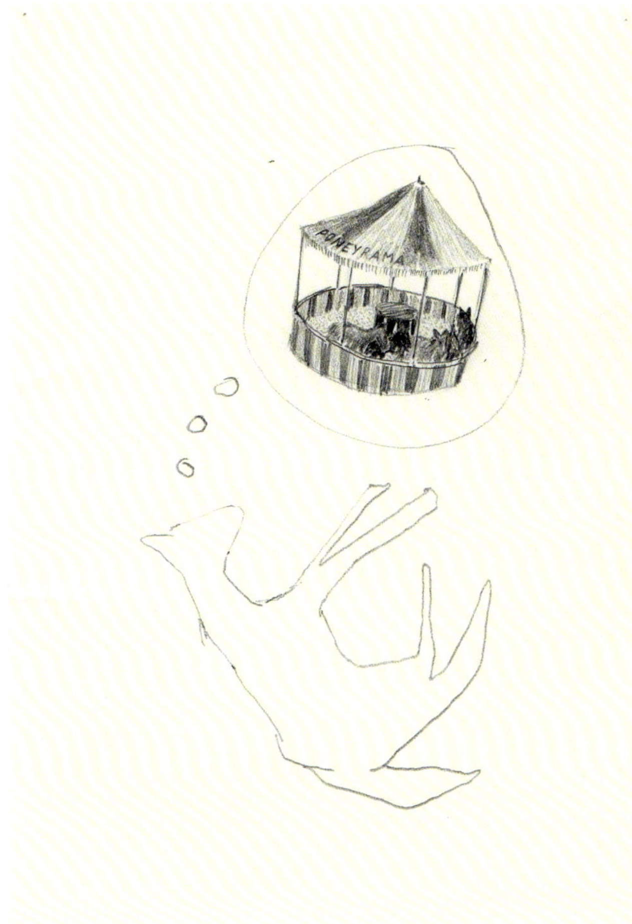

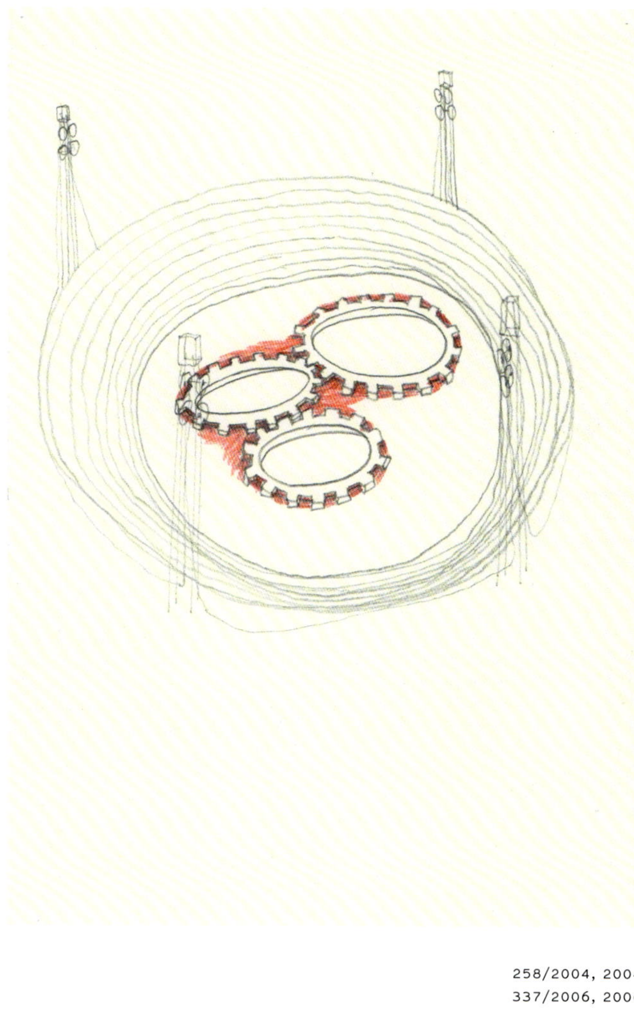

258/2004, 2004
337/2006, 2006

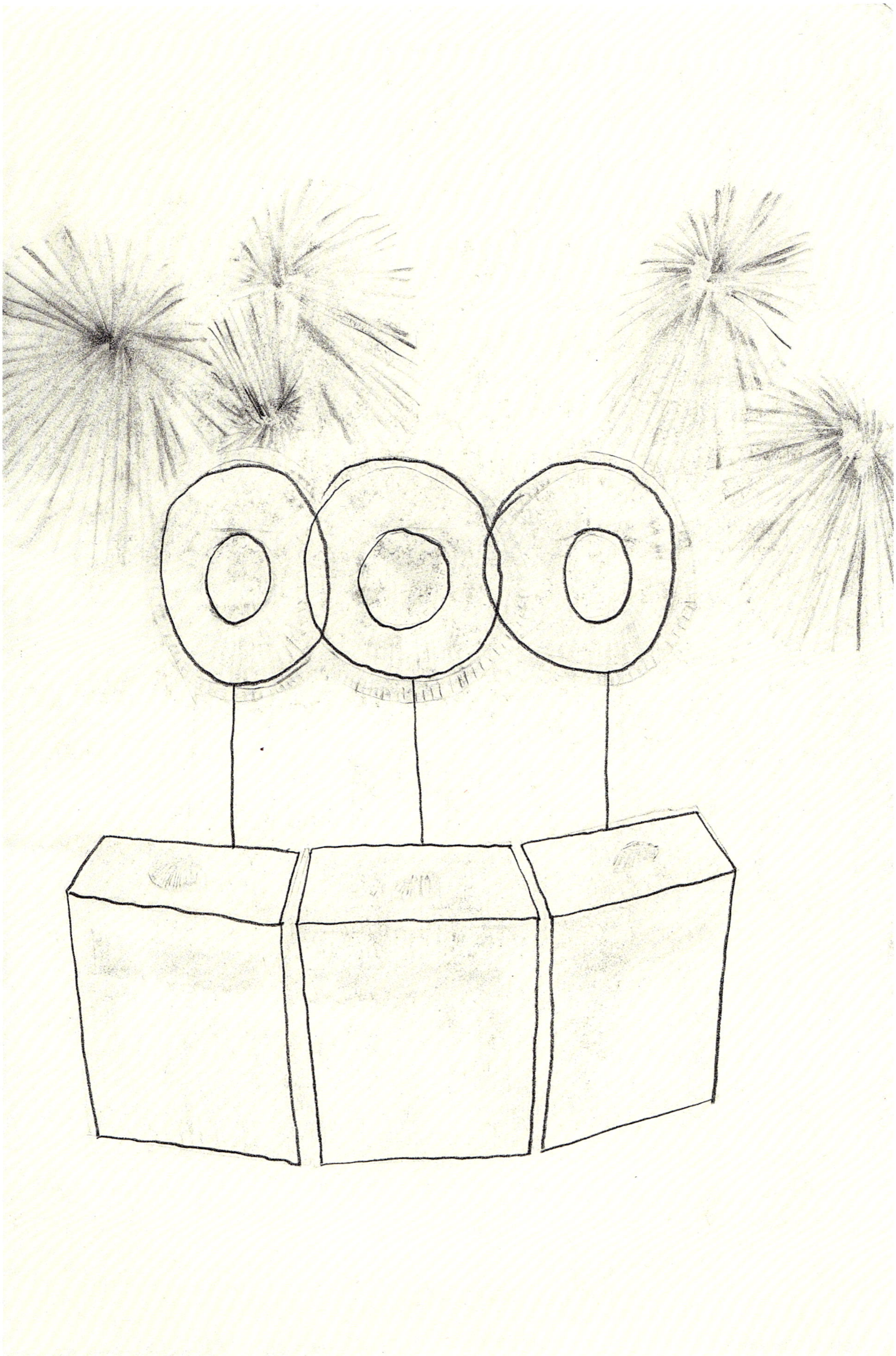

266/2004, 2004

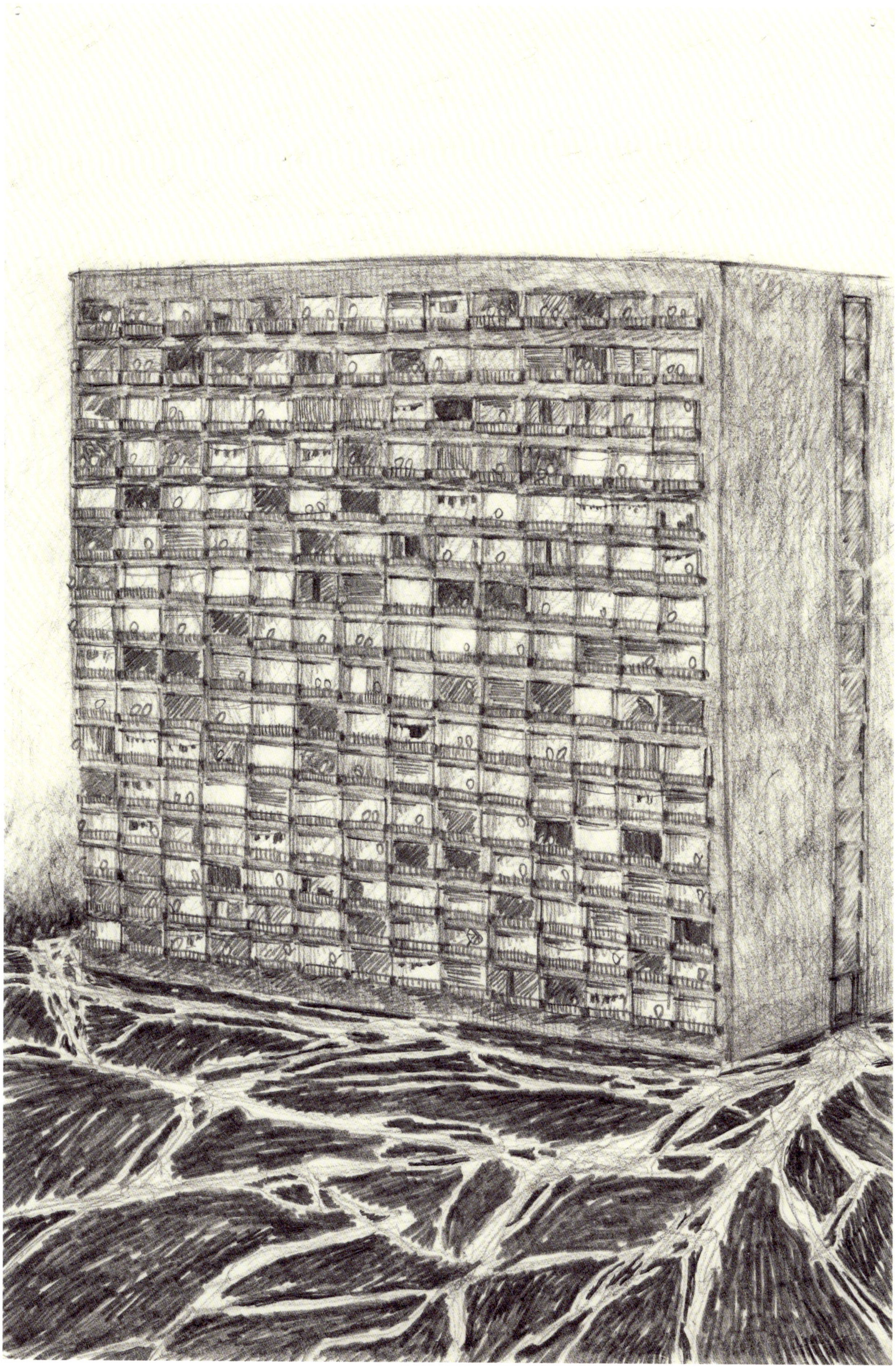

326/2006, 2006

324/2006, 2006

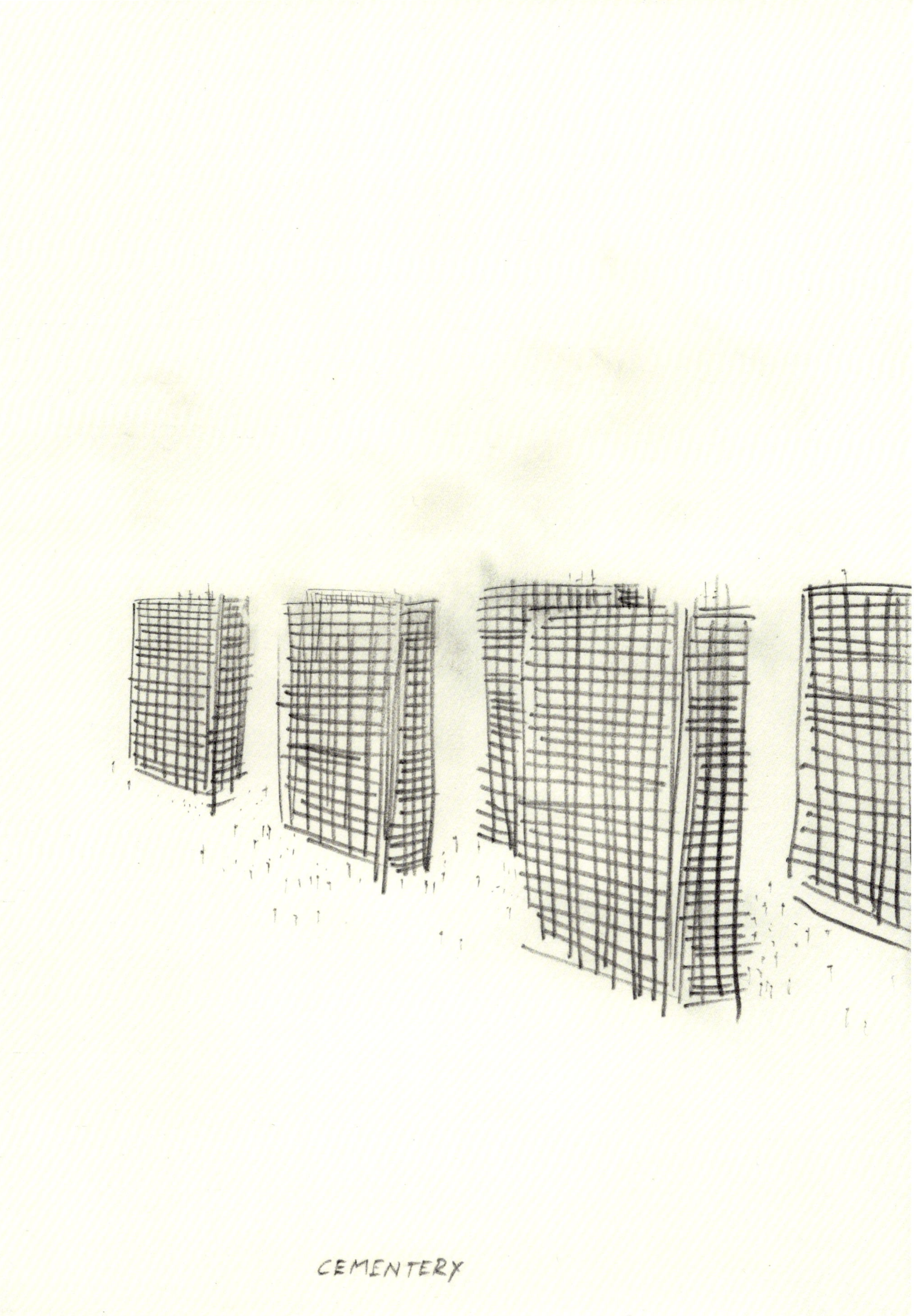

358/2007, 2007

368/2007, 2007

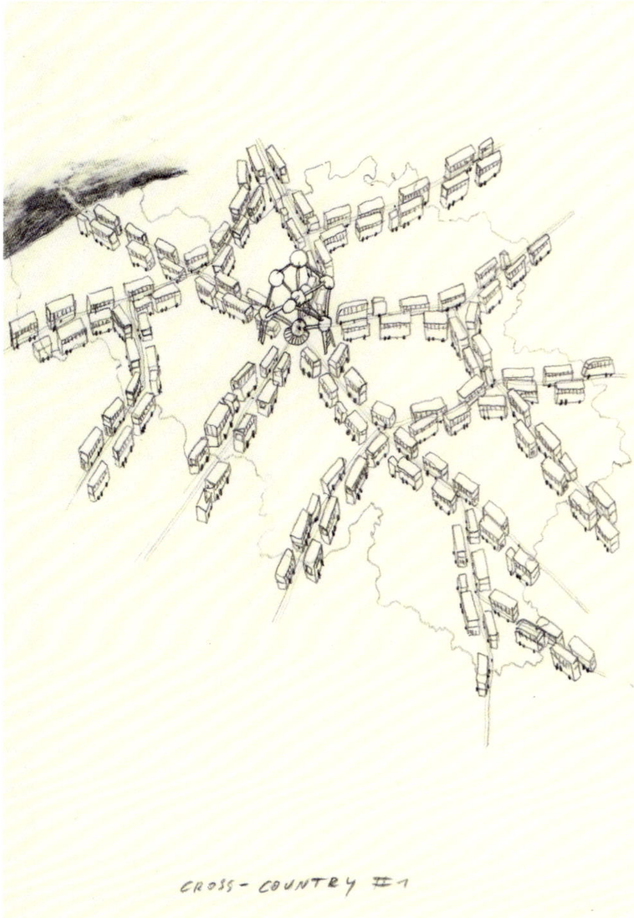

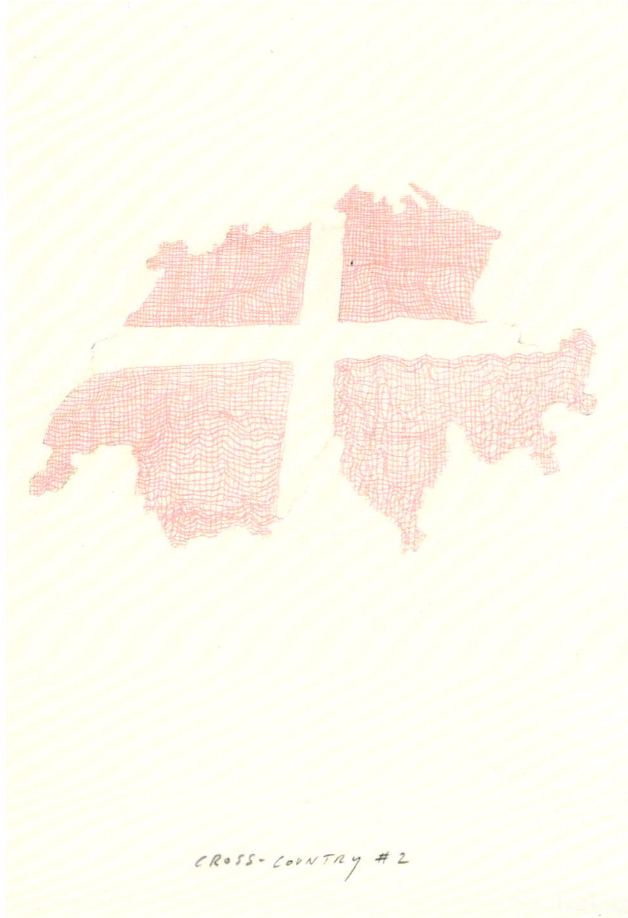

384/2008, 2008
385/2008, 2008

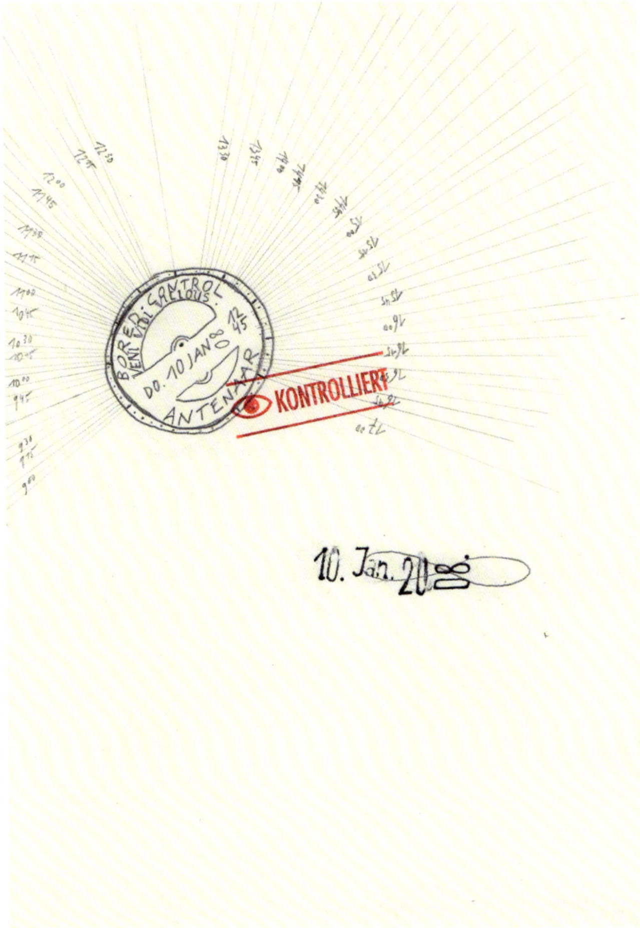

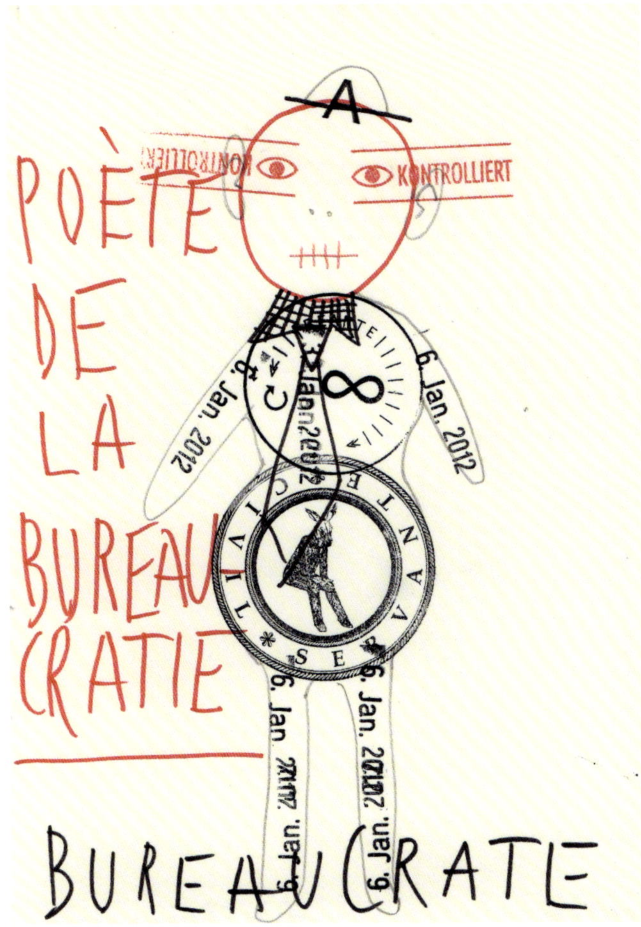

372/2008, 2008
566/2012, 2012

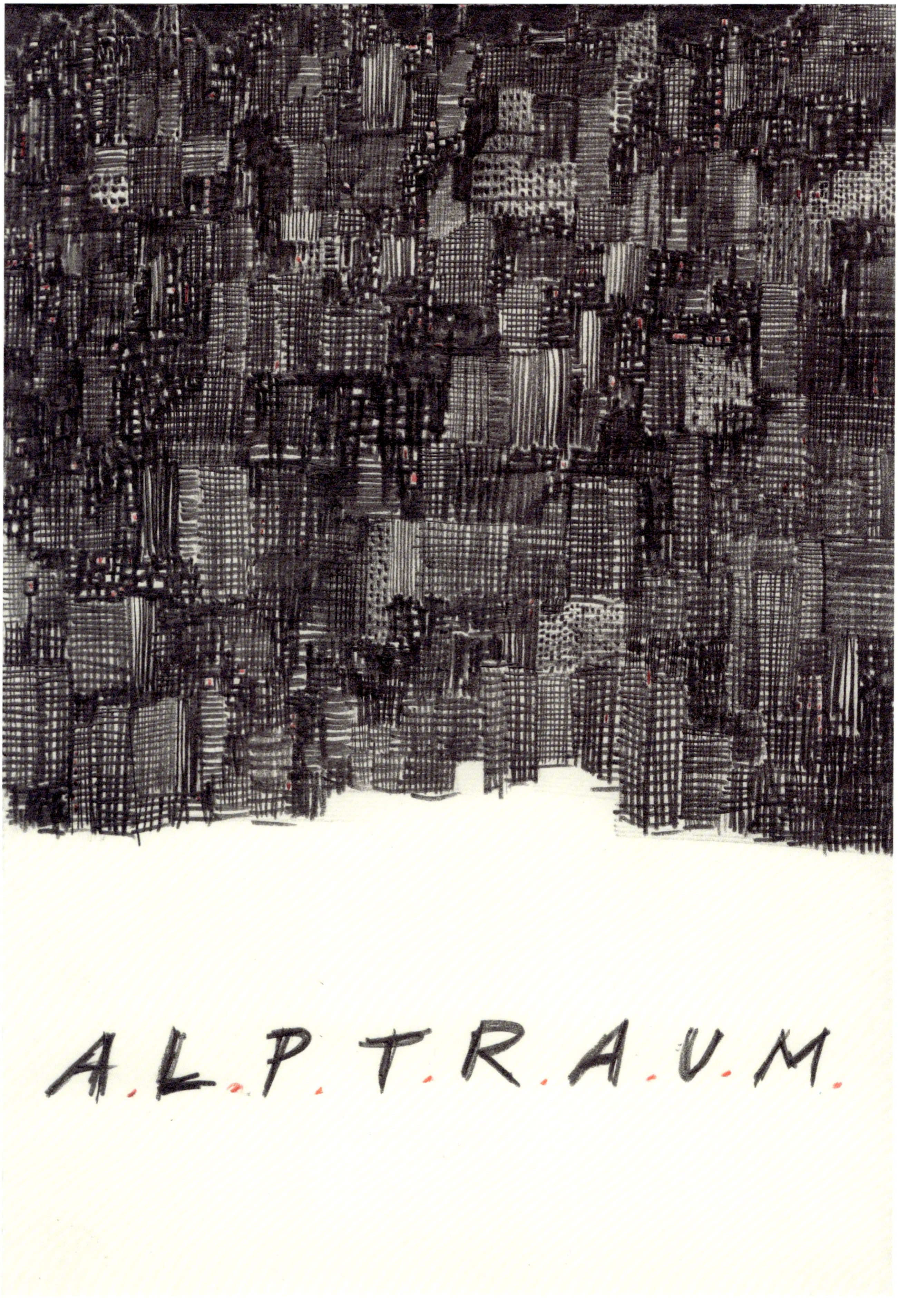

411/2008, 2008

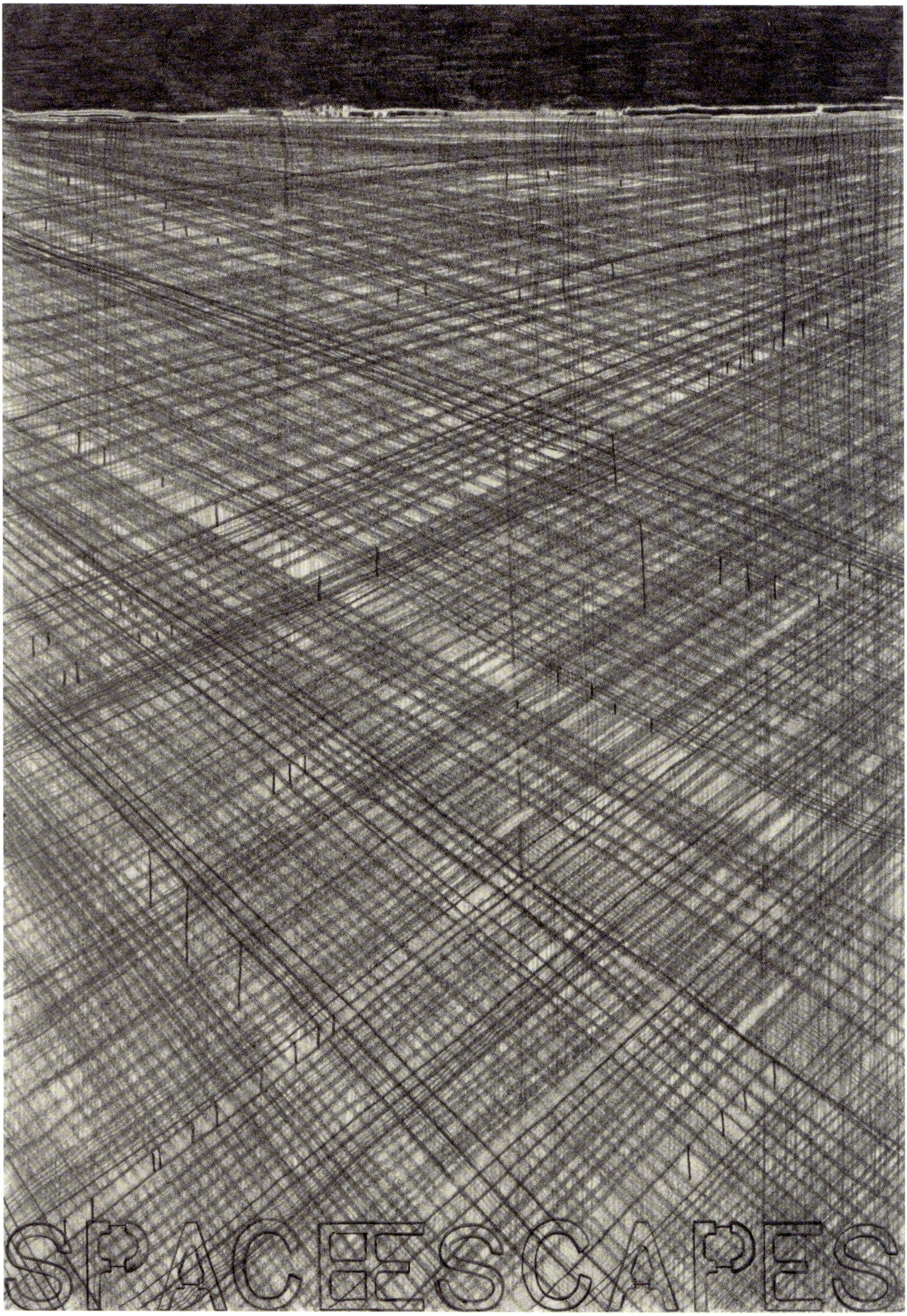

410/2008, 2008

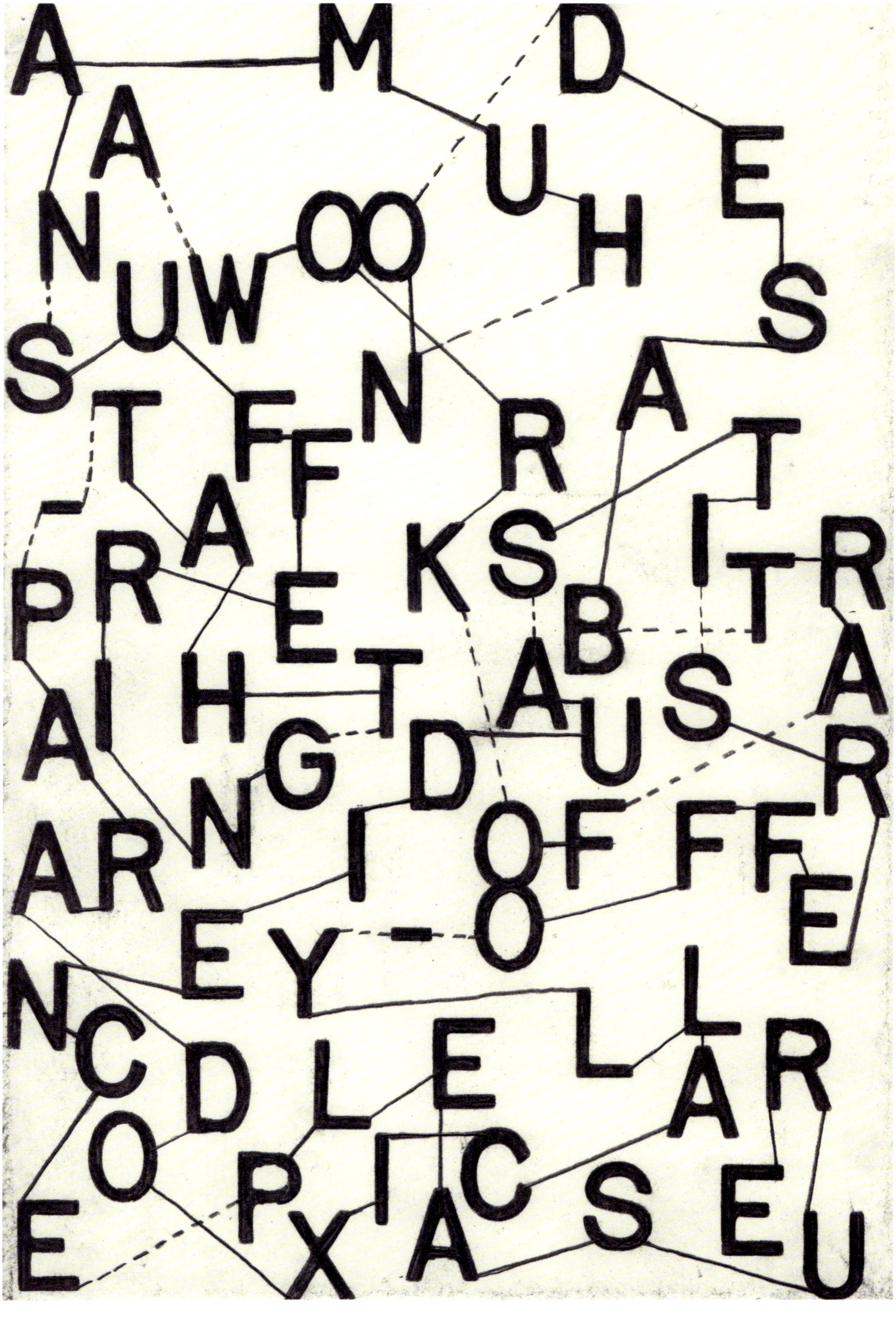

463/2009, 2009

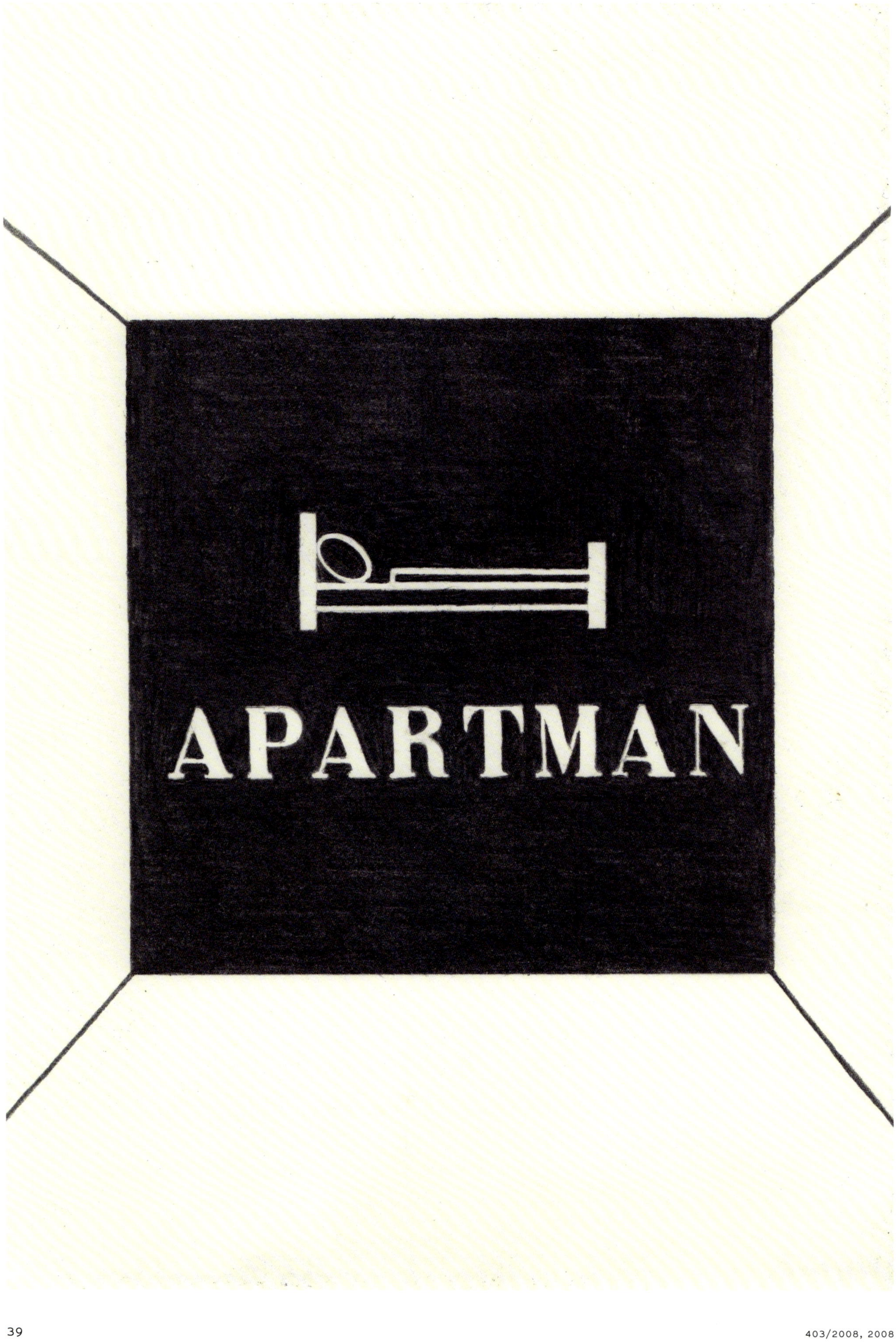

403/2008, 2008

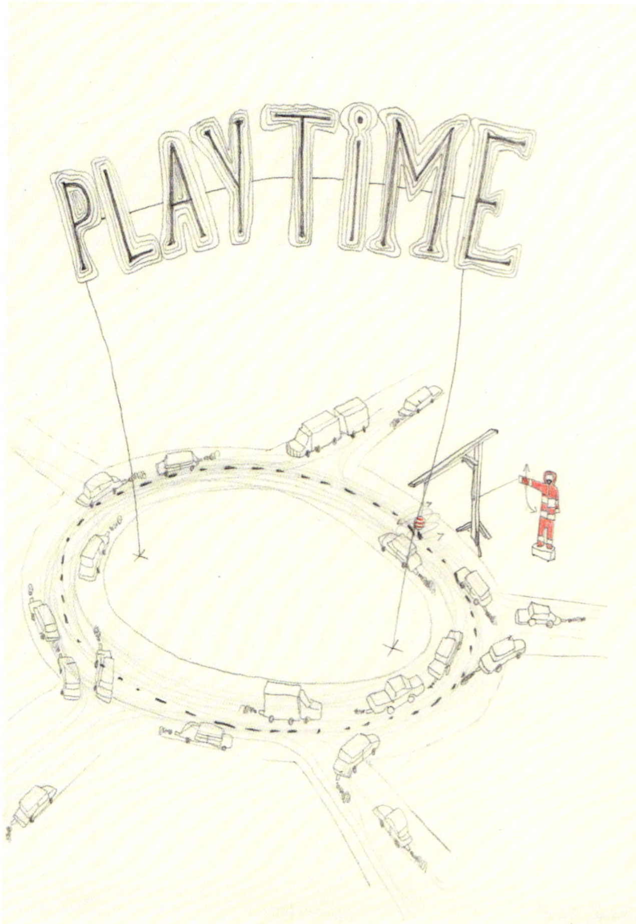

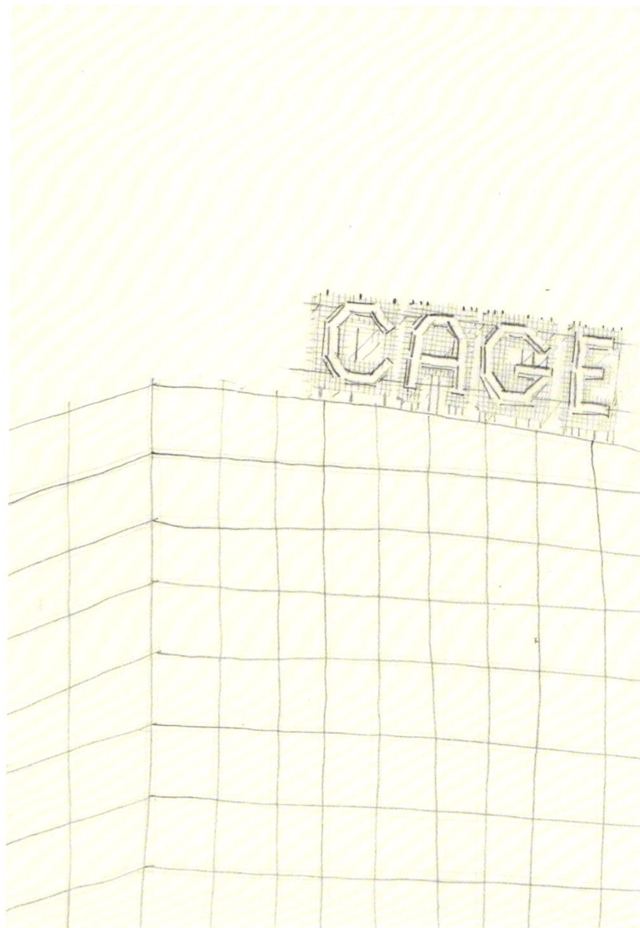

374/2008, 2008
376/2008, 2008

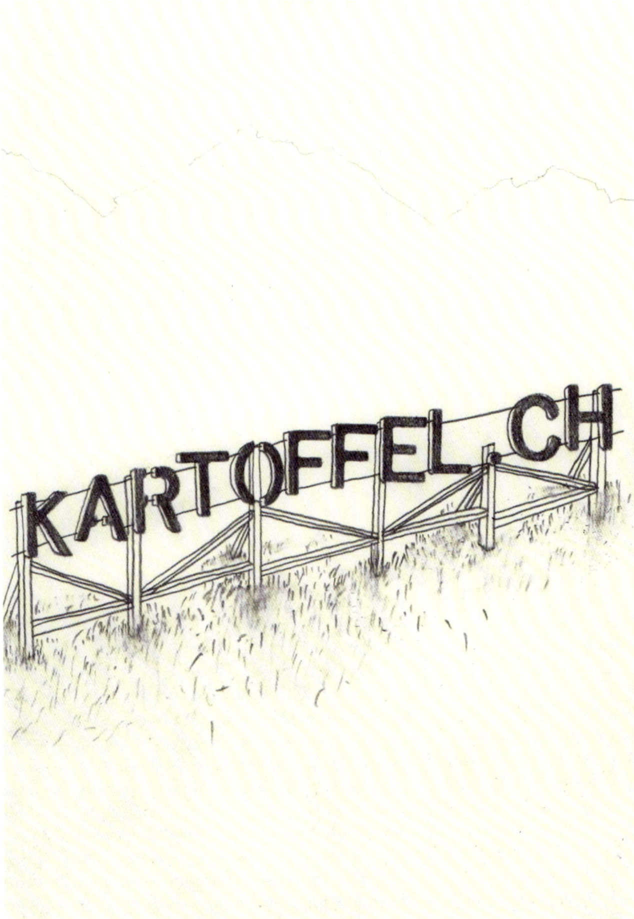

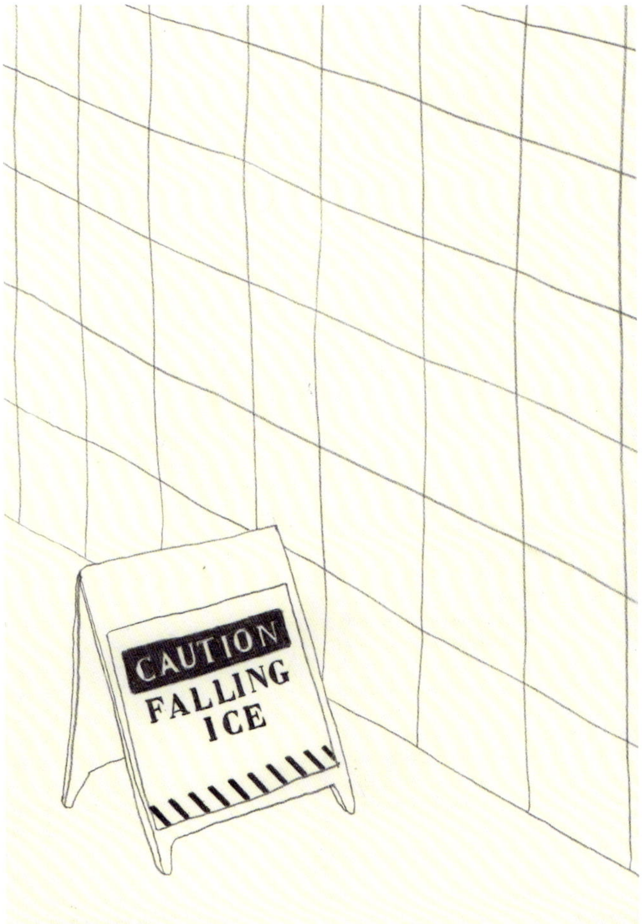

462/2009, 2009
422/2009, 2009

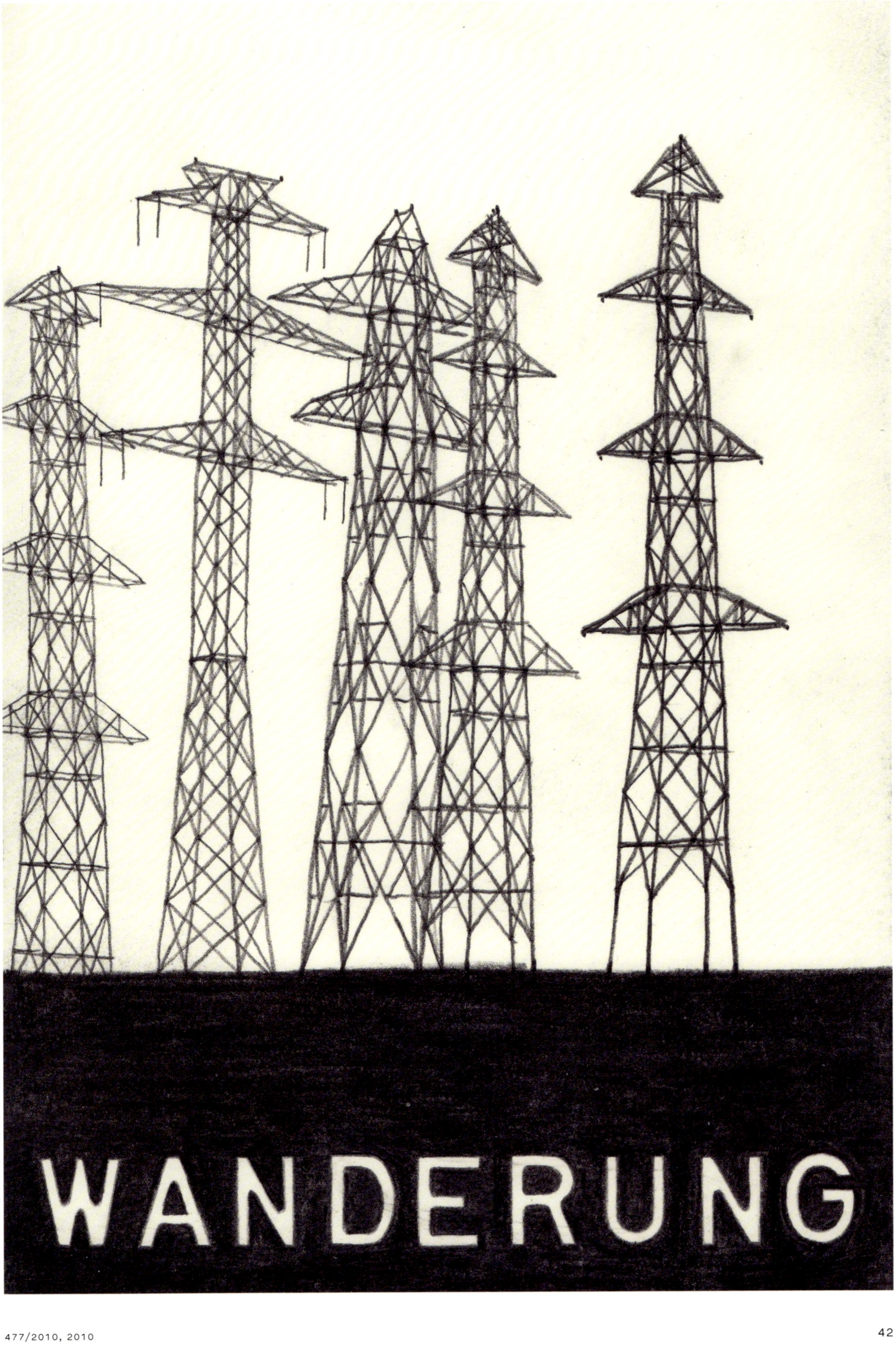

477/2010, 2010

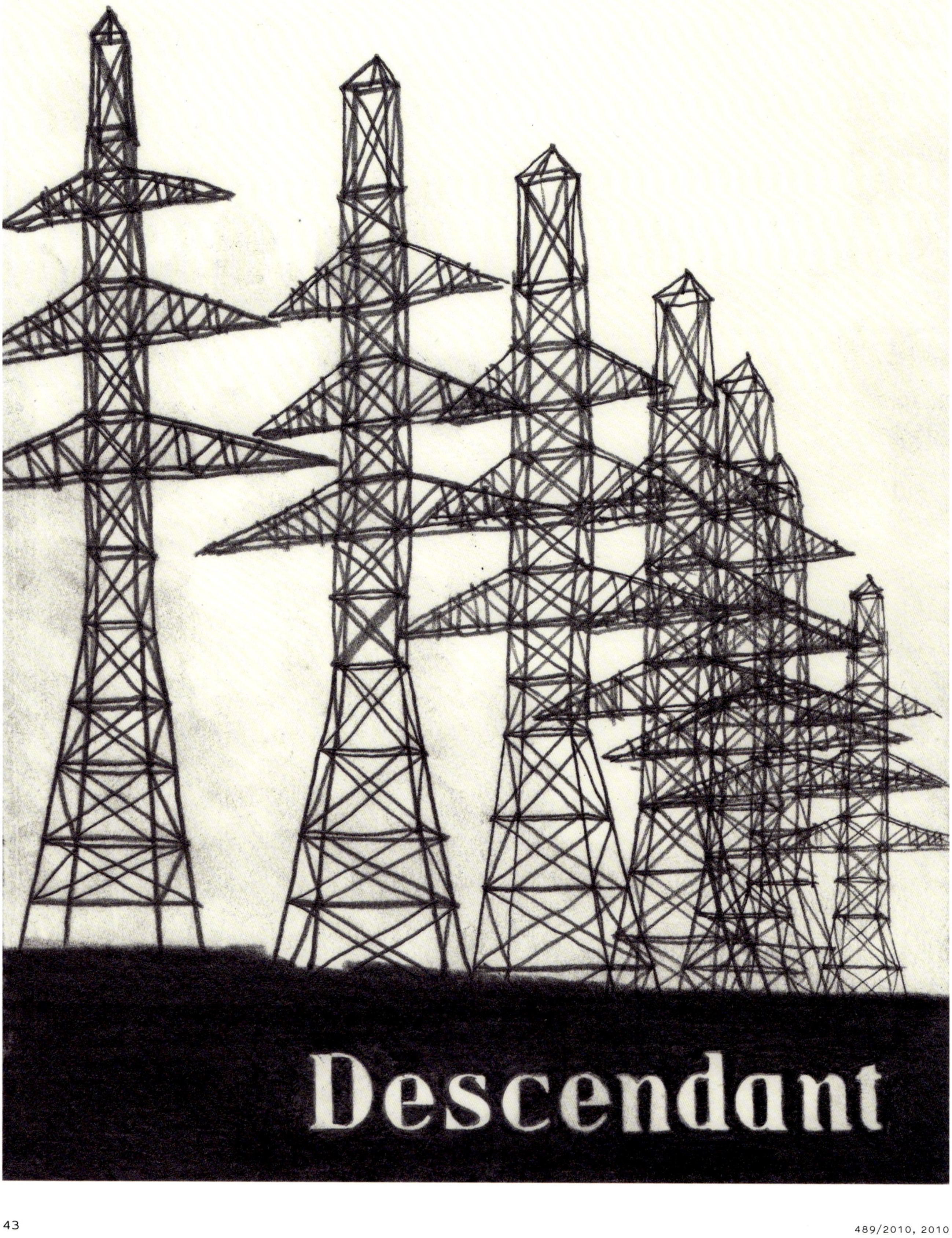

489/2010, 2010

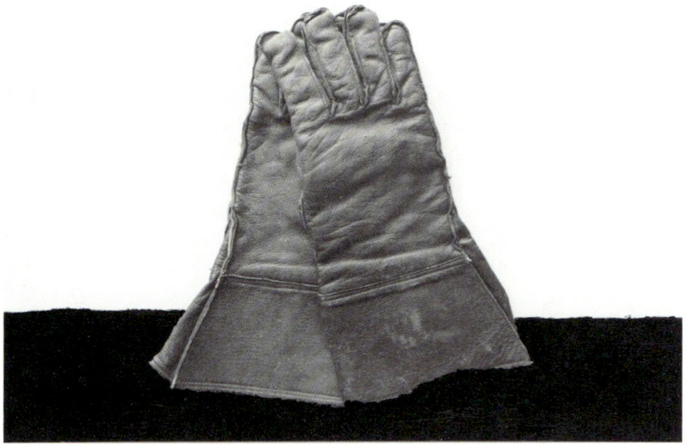

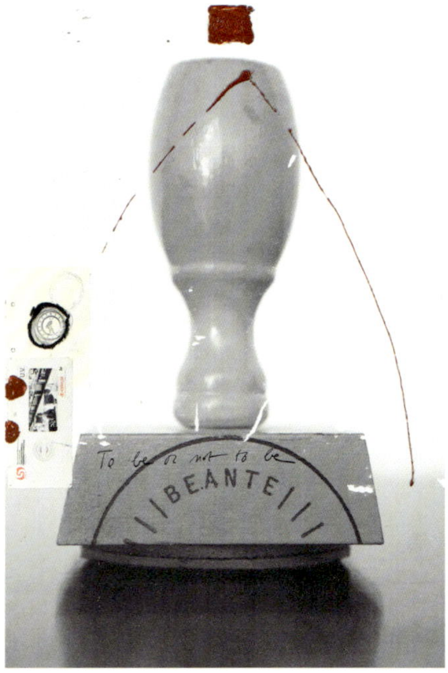

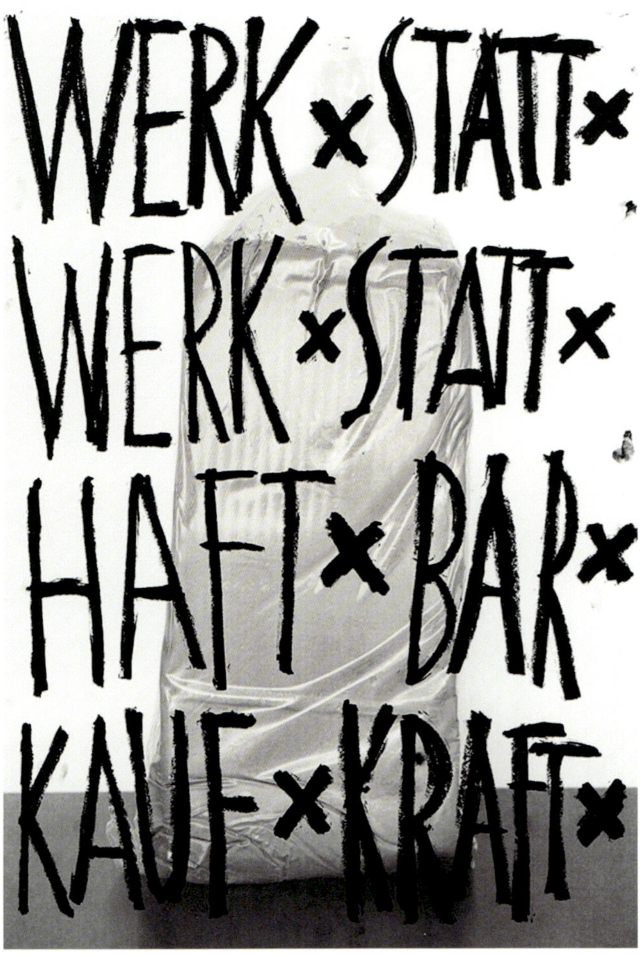

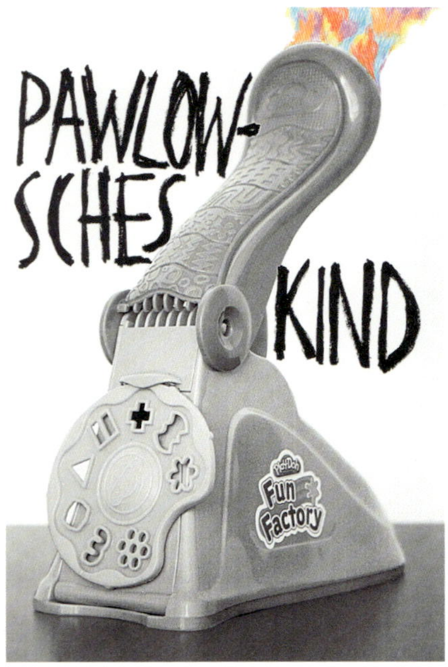

NR.4(SISYPHOS), 2012
NR.8(BEANTE), 2012
NR.3(WERK-KRAFT), 2012
NR.7(PAWLOW), 2012

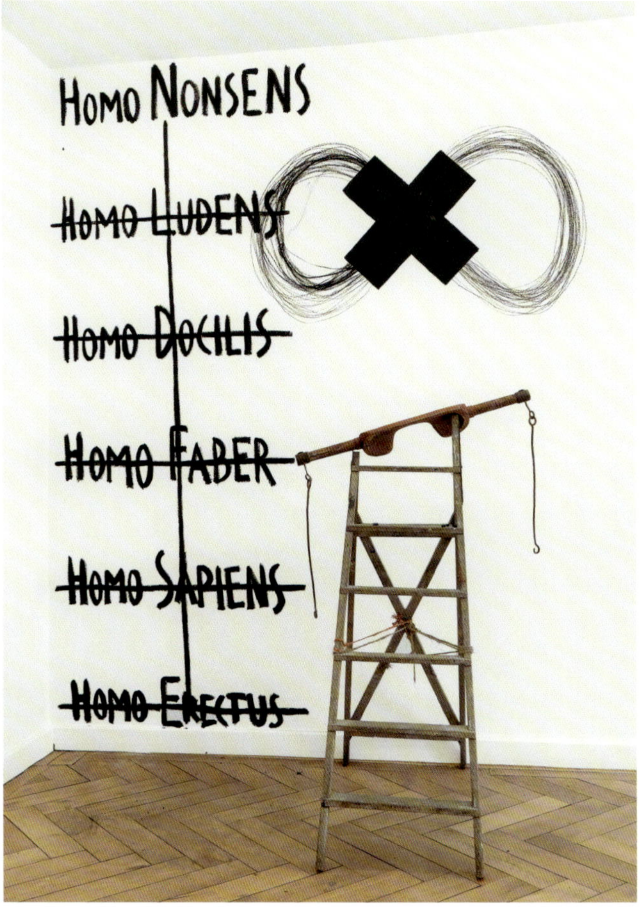

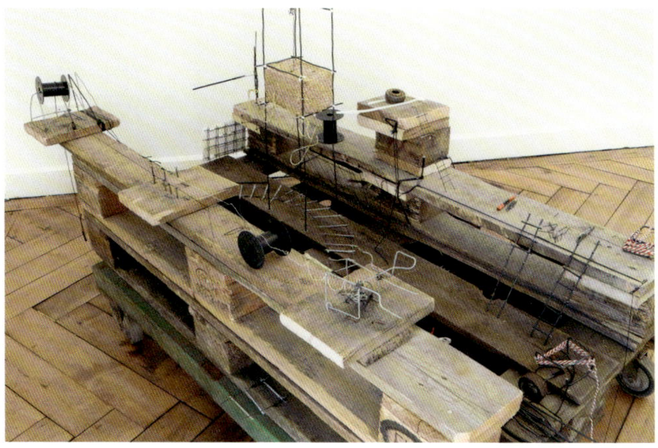

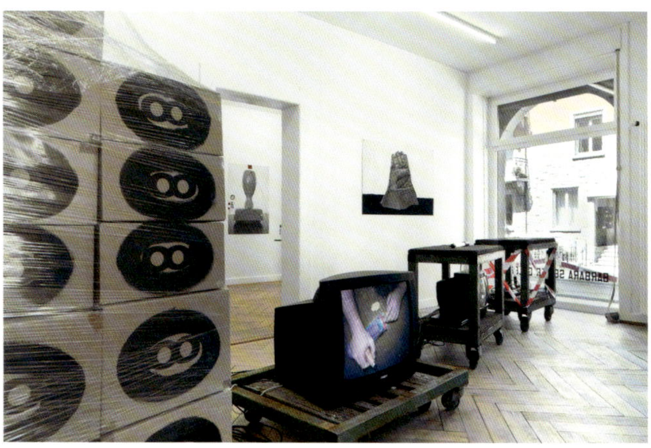

WERK STATT WERK,
GALERIE BARBARA SEILER, ZURICH, 2012

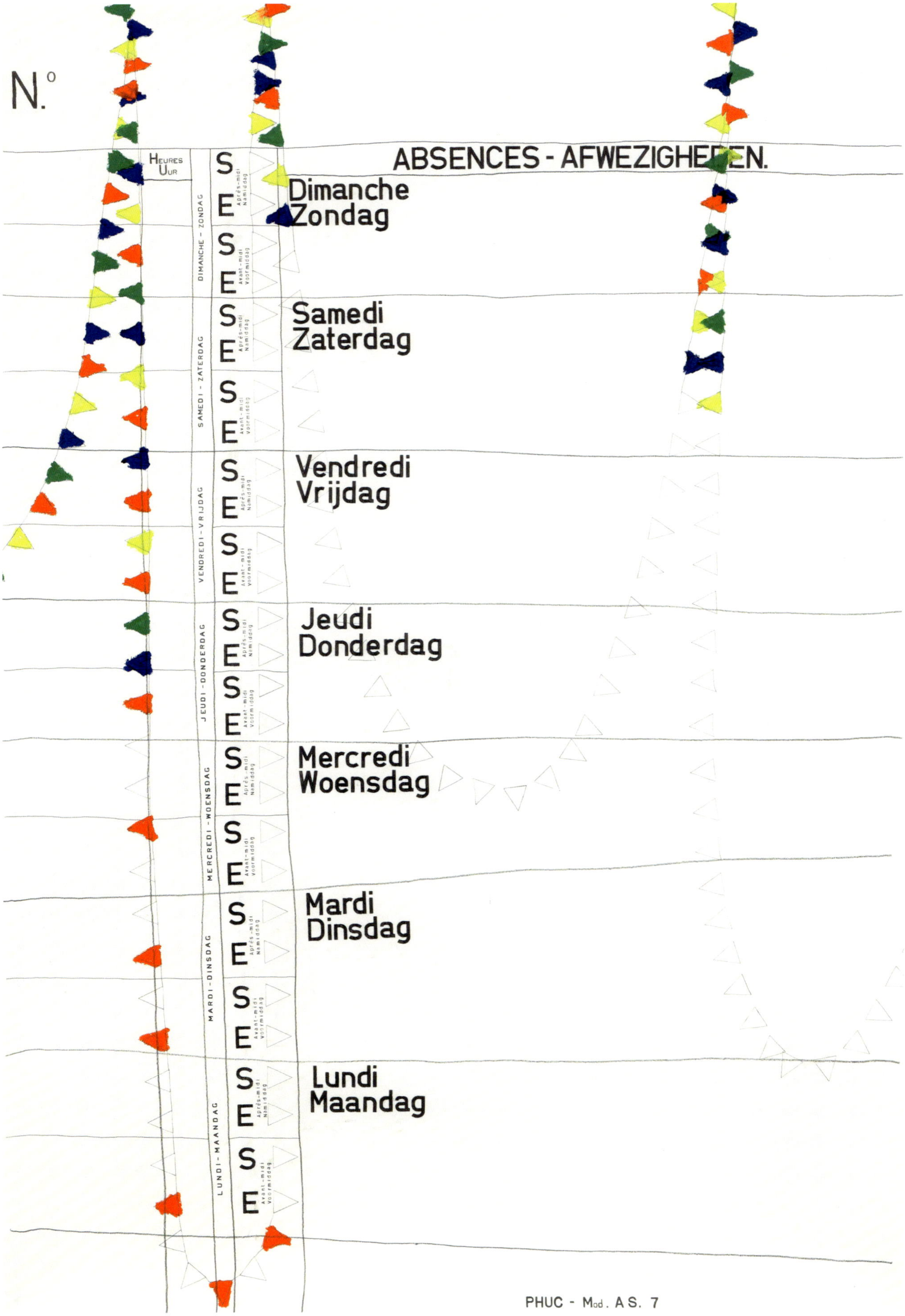

STECHKARTE (POESIE DER LANGEWEILE), 2010

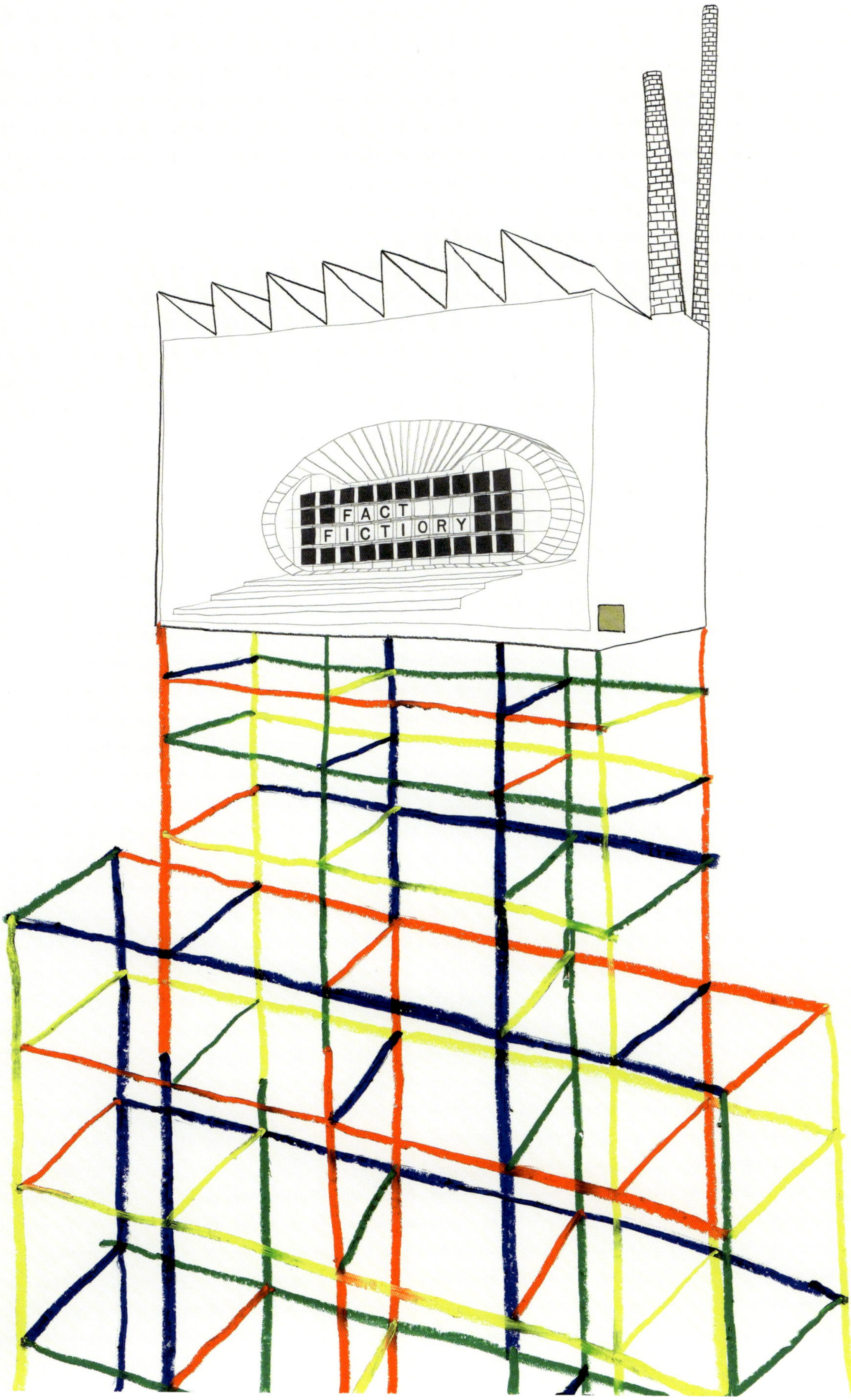

FICTIORY (POESIE DER LANGEWEILE), 2010

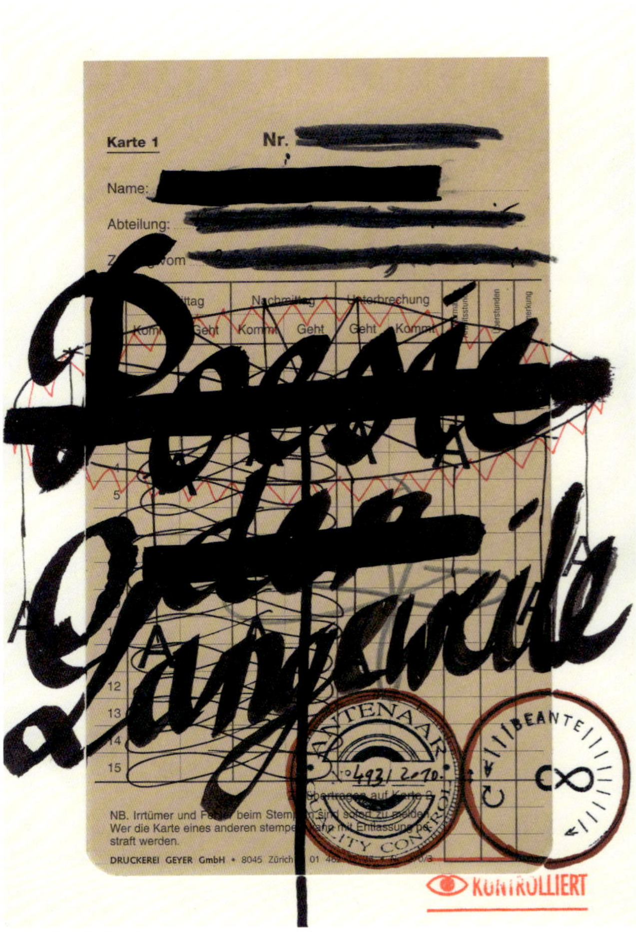

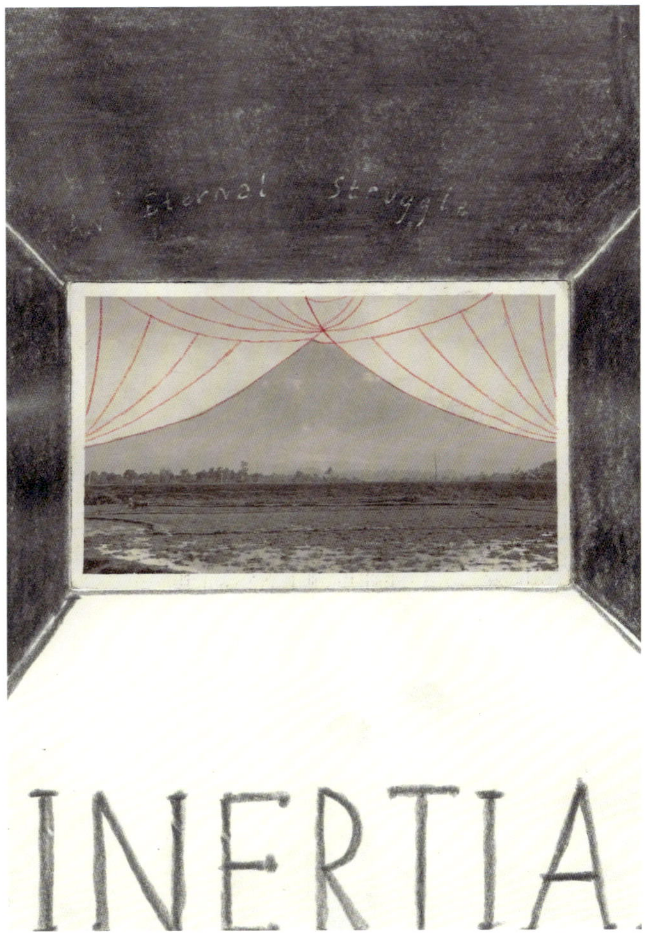

493/2010, 2010
500/2010, 2010

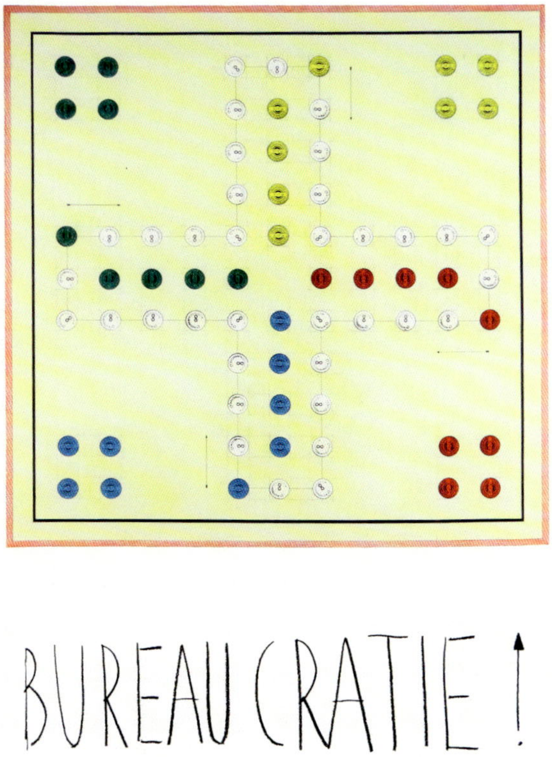

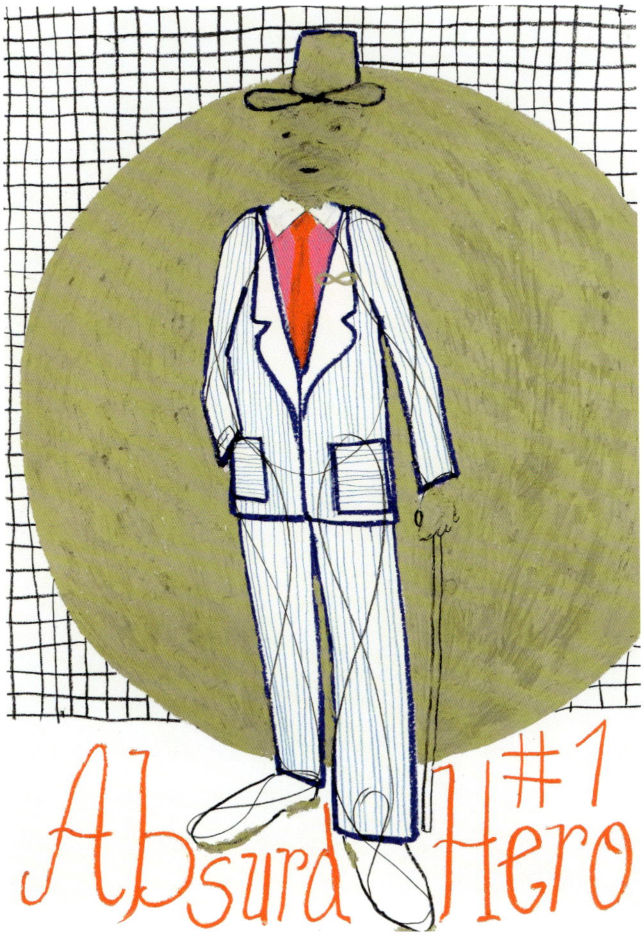

BUREAUCRATIE (0-99 JAAR), 2011
ABSURD HERO#1 (POESIE DER LANGEWEILE), 2010

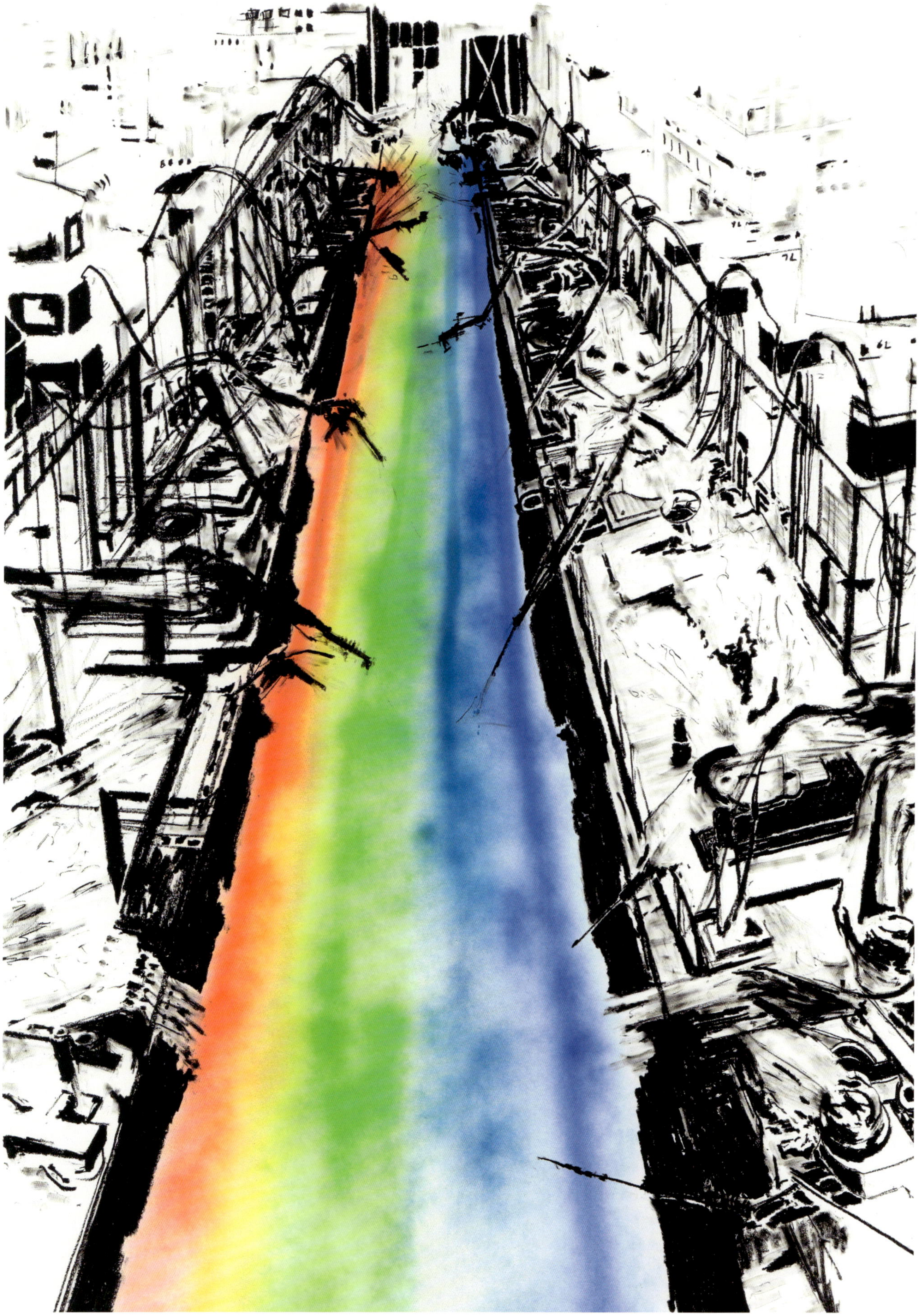

PRODUCTION LINE, 2011

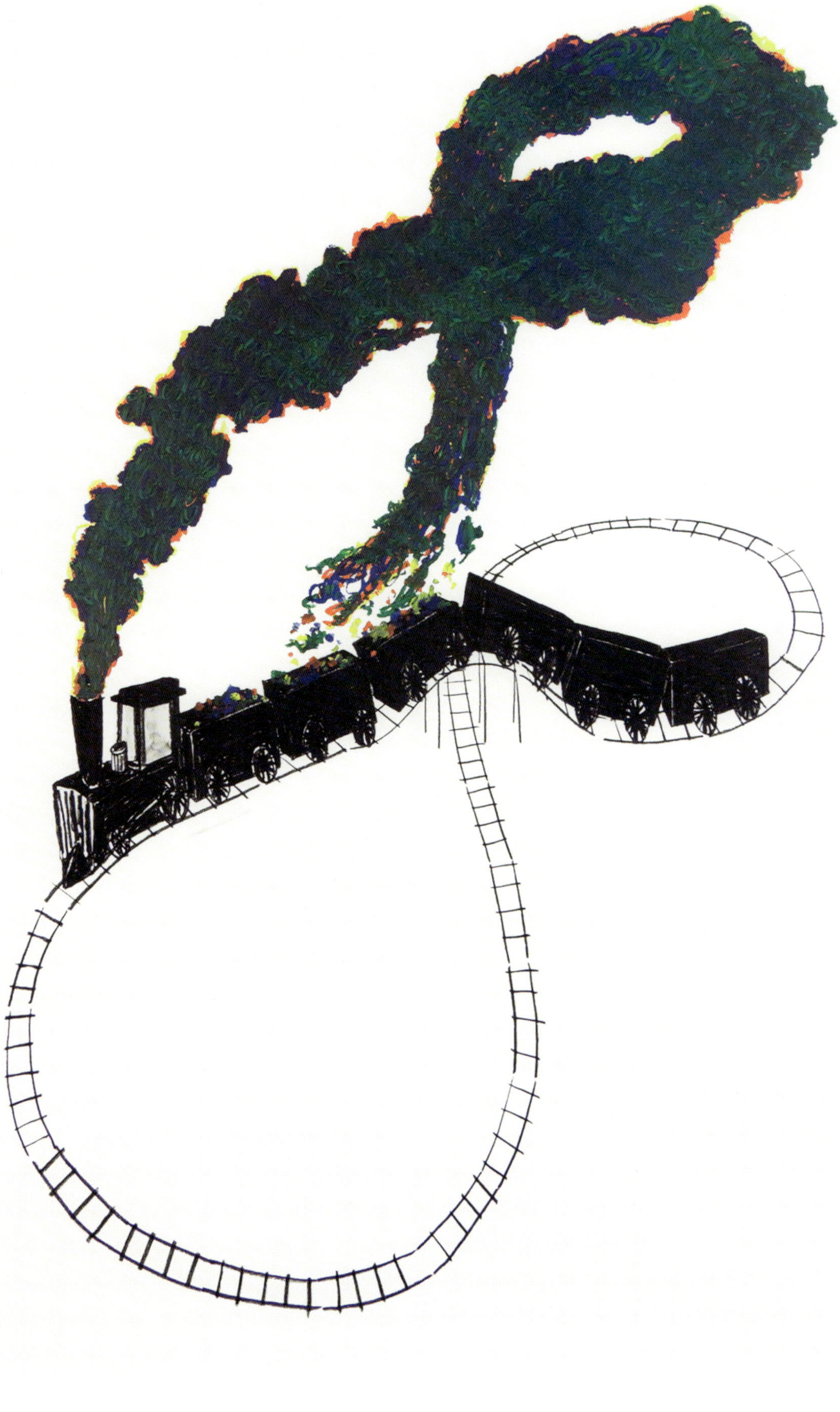

CHEMIN DE LA VIE, 2011

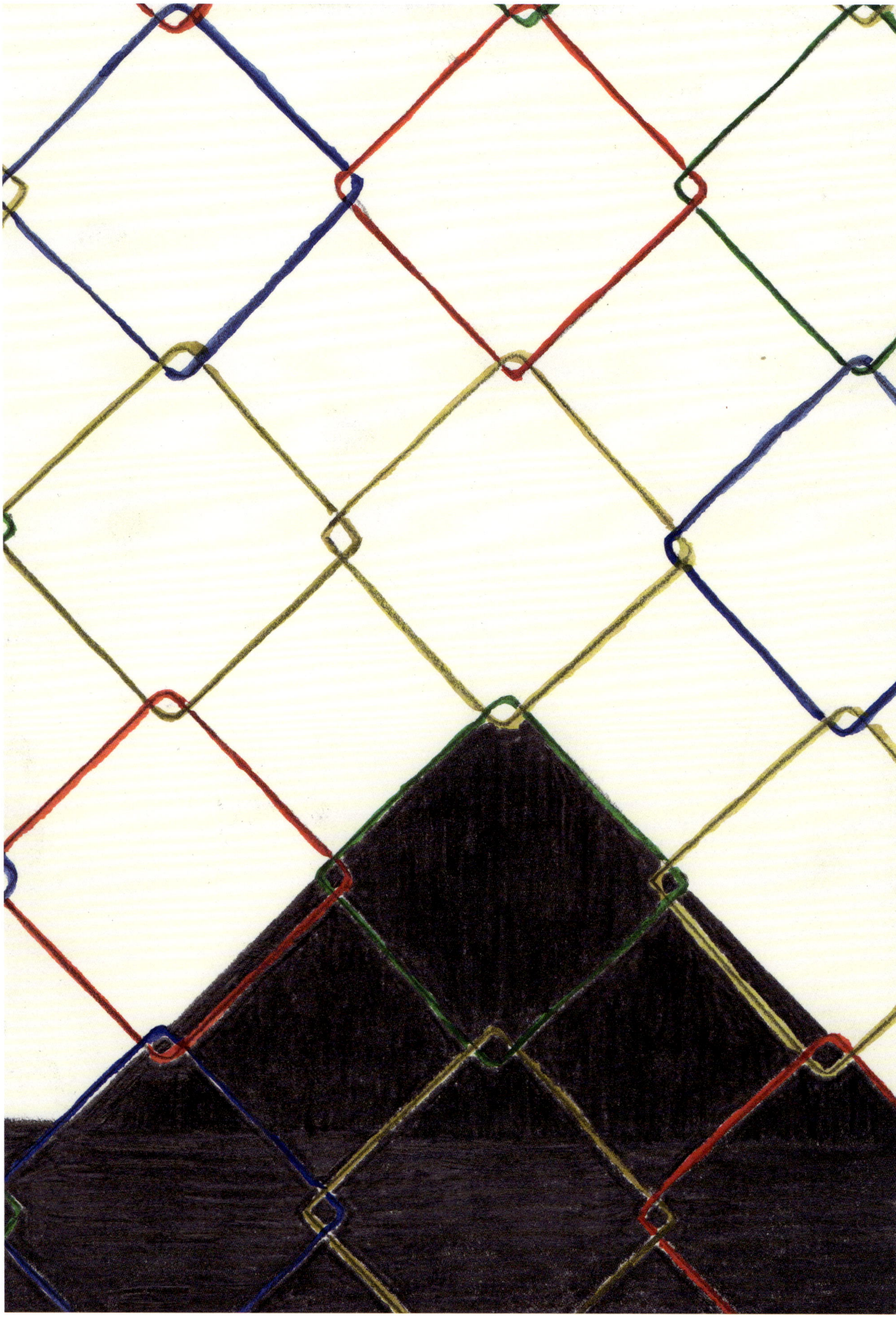

527/2011, 2011

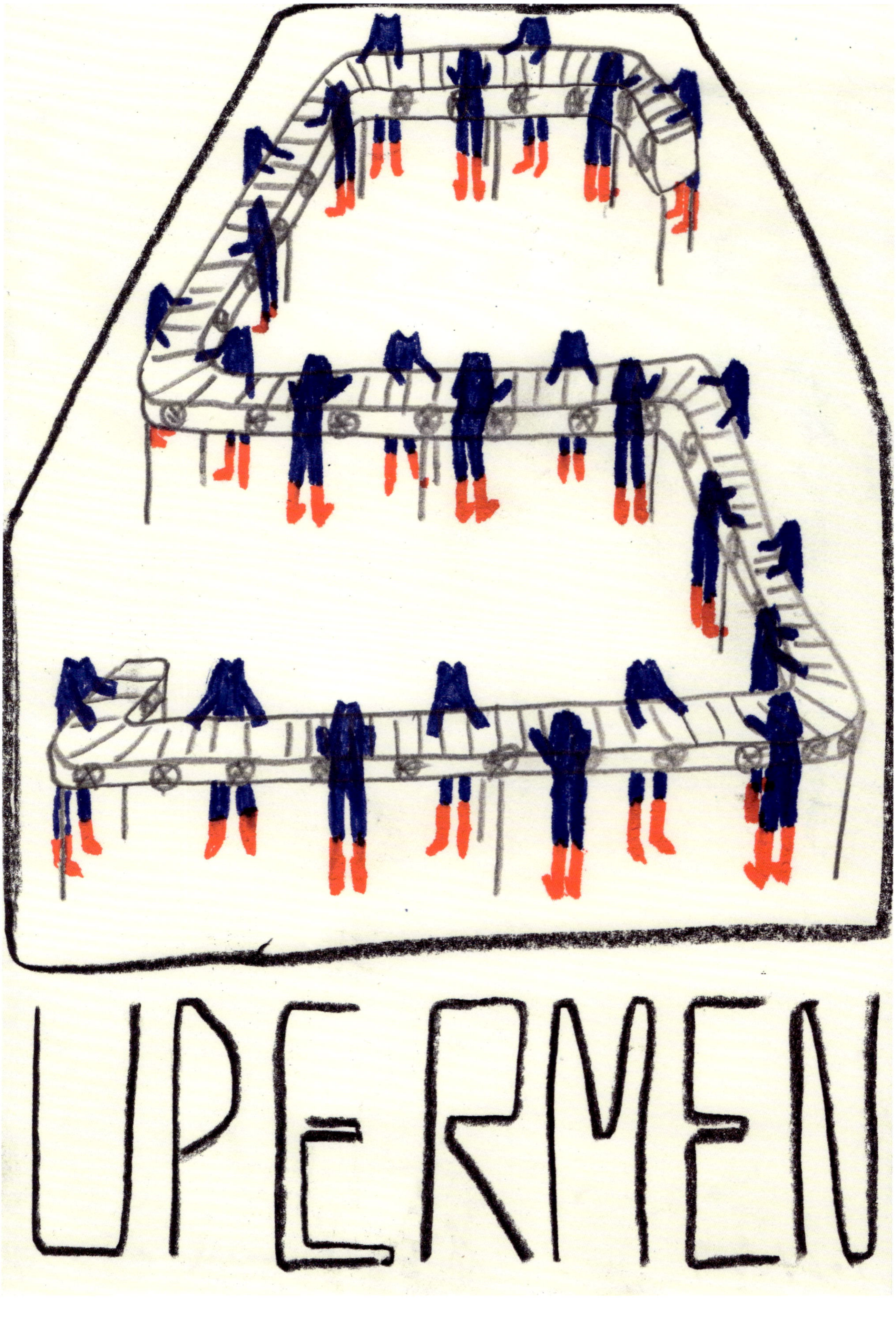

506/2011, 2011

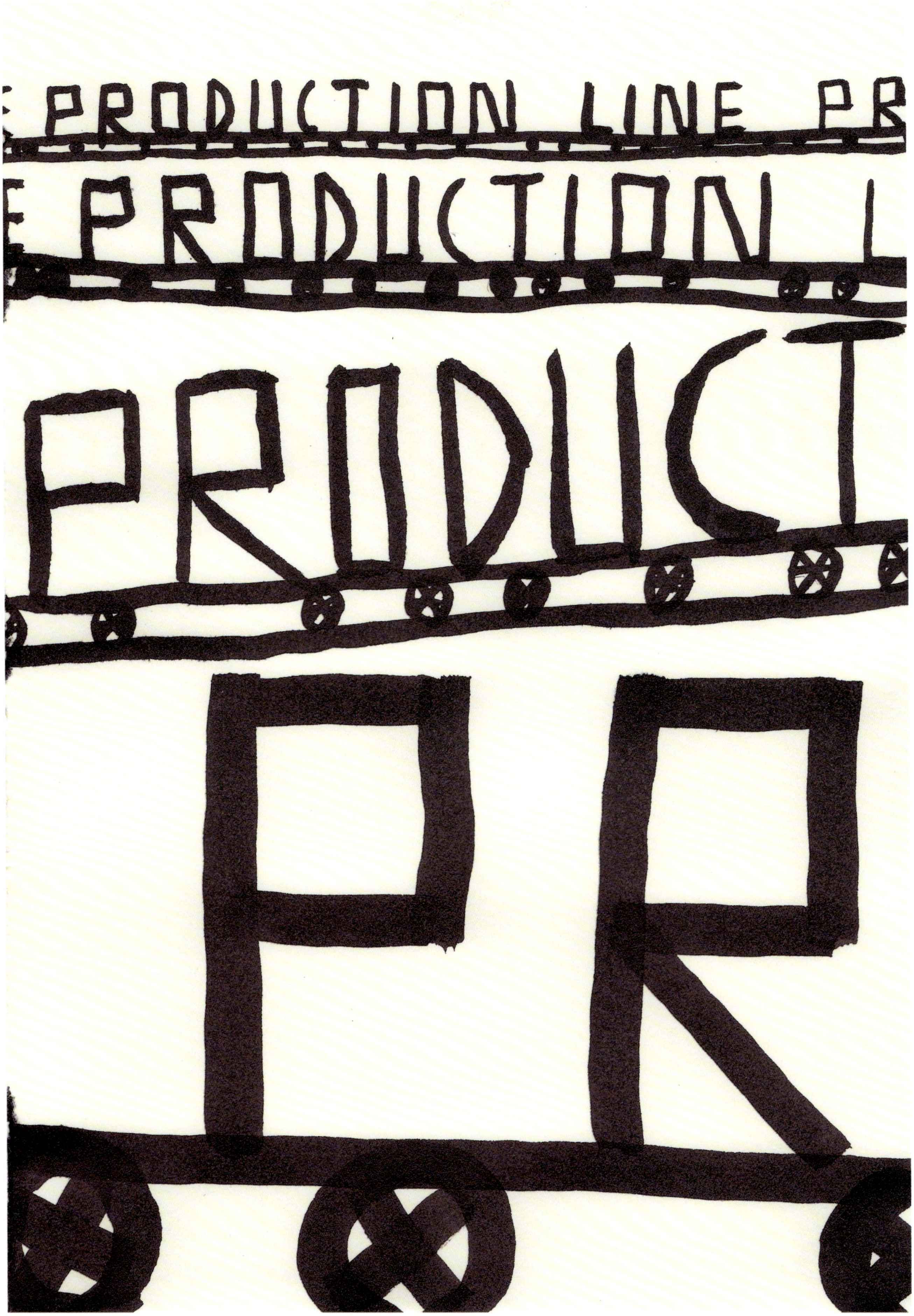

516/2011, 2011

547/2011, 2011
549/2011, 2011

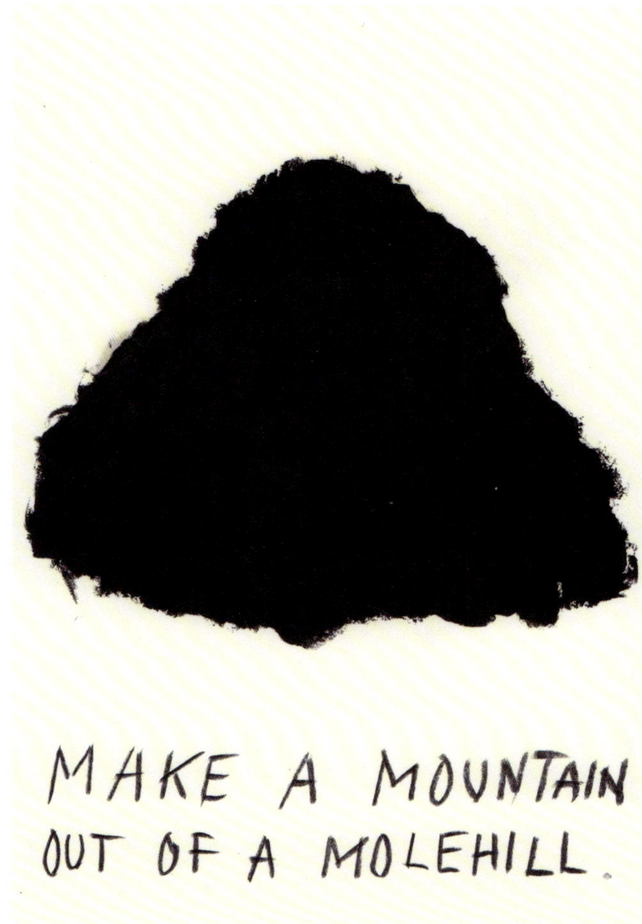

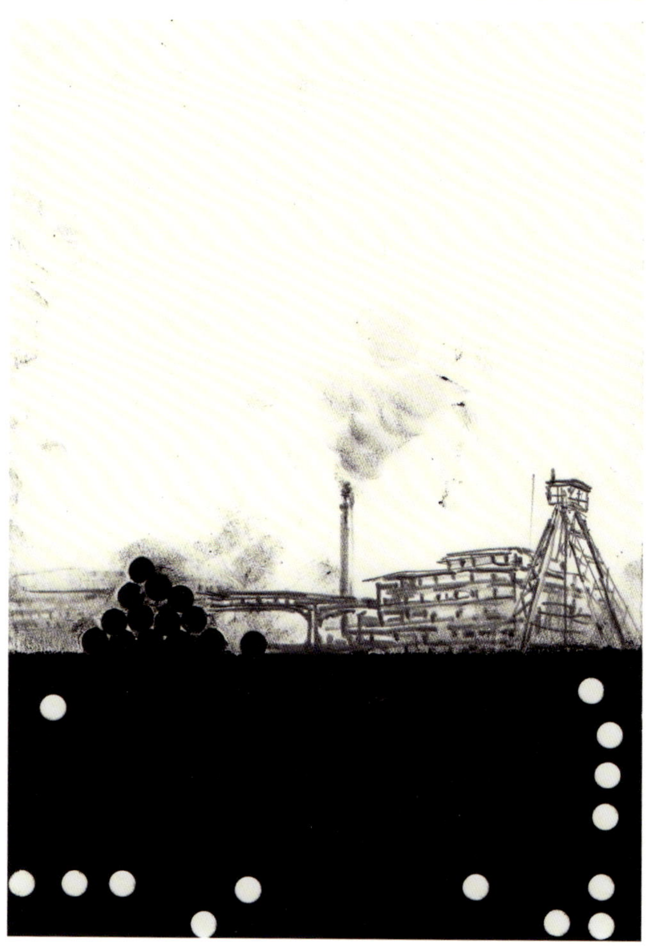

548/2011, 2011
568/2012, 2012

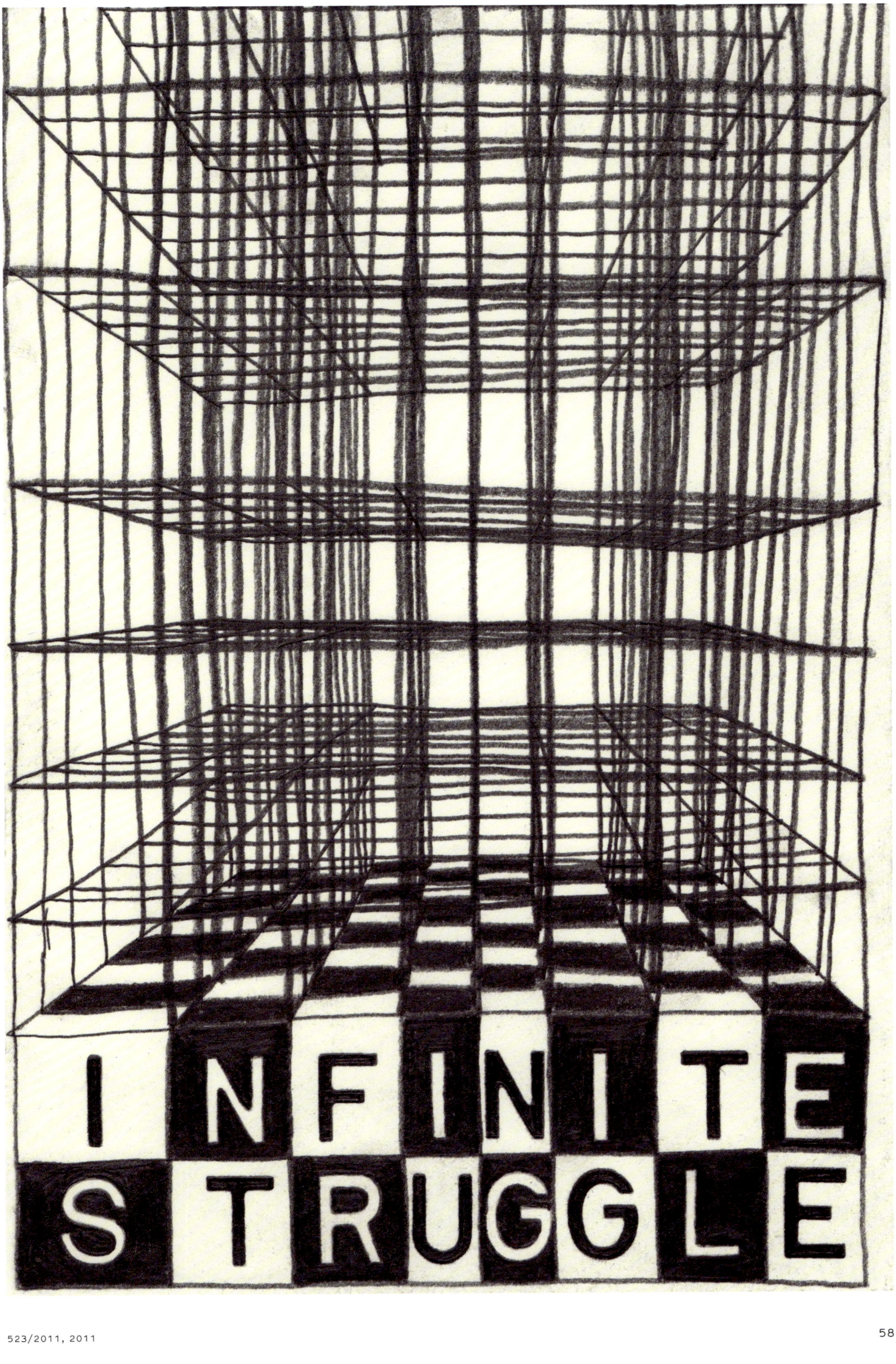

523/2011, 2011

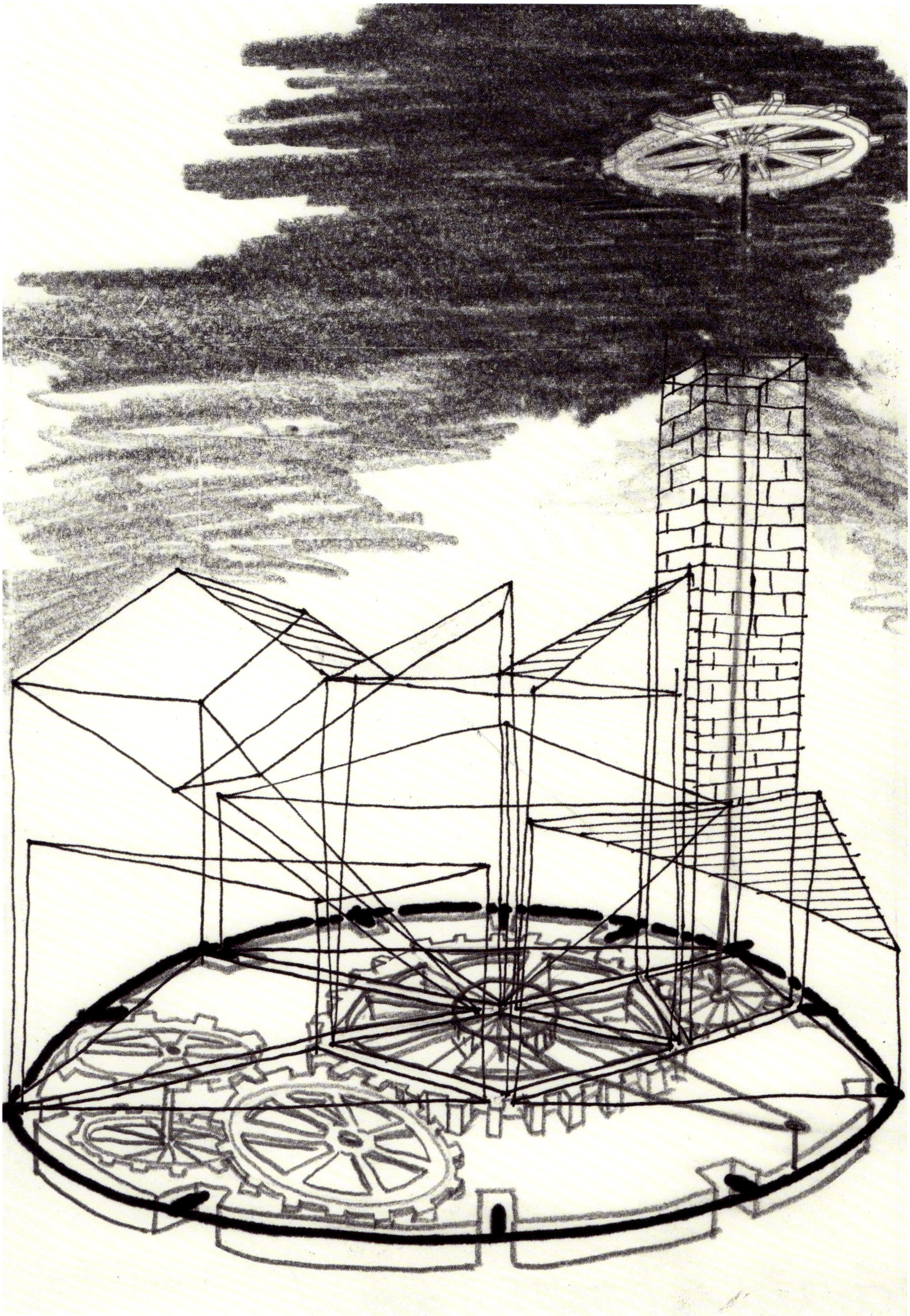

514/2011, 2011

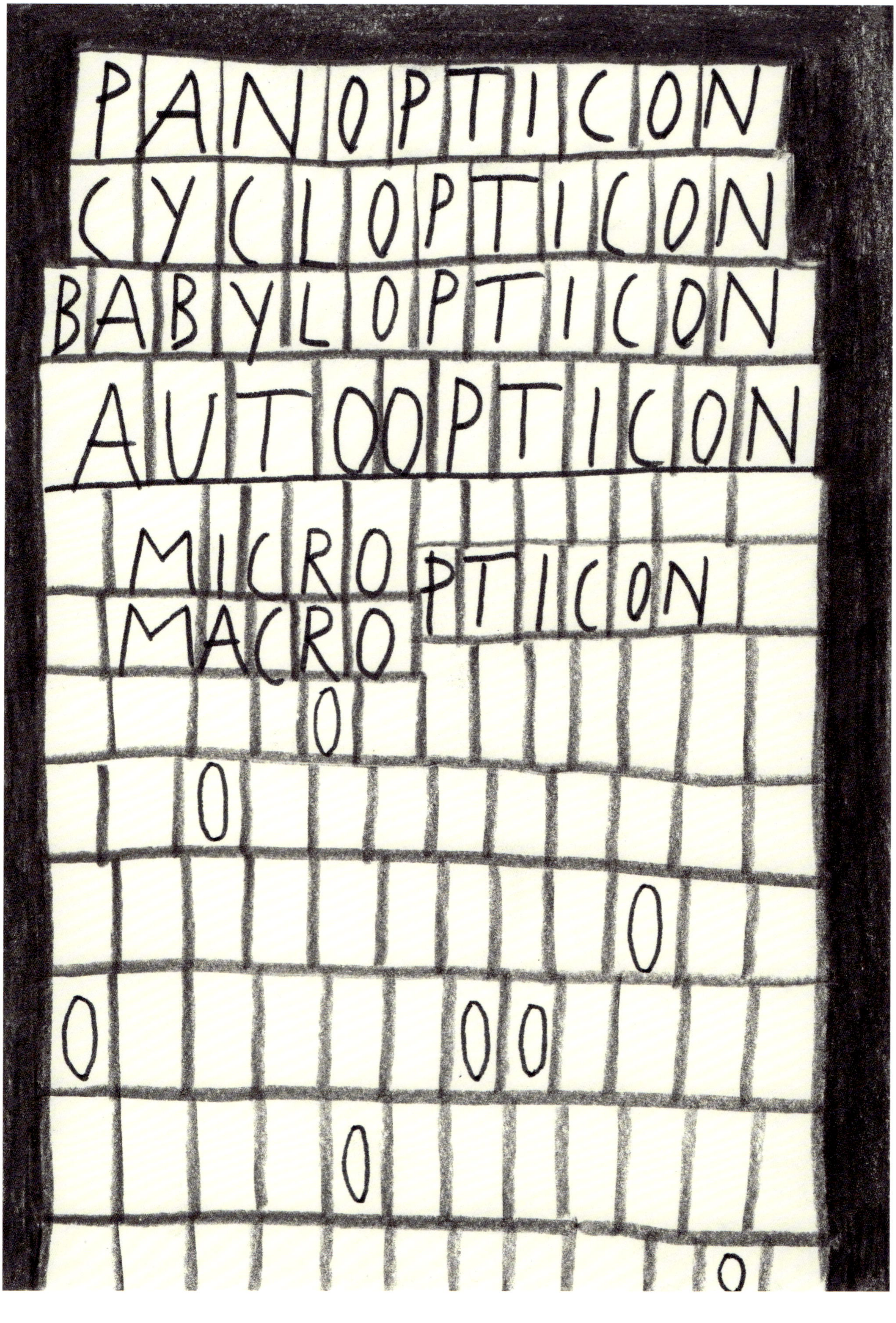

474/2010, 2010

List of Works

[p. 3] #22/2009 (UNTITLED), 2009
Chalkboard paint and chalk on paperboard, 130 × 100 cm
Courtesy the artist

[p. 4] 398/2008, 2008
Pencil on paper, 21.2 × 14.5 cm
Private collection, Starnberg

[p. 5] 400/2008, 2008
Pencil on paper, 21.2 × 14.5 cm
Private collection

[p. 6] #5/2010 (SEVERAL THOUGHTS), 2010
Chalk and wax crayon on paper, 29.7 × 20.9 cm
Private collection, Brussels

[p. 11] #2/2010 (FABRICATION), 2010
Pencil on paper, 210 × 154 cm
Private collection, Bruges

[p. 12] MAKE A MOLEHILL OUT OF A MOUNTAIN (OF WORK), installation views of *The Deep of the Modern*, *Manifesta 9*, Genk, 2012

[p. 21] 58/2002, 2002
Pencil and felt-tip pen on paper, 22.4 × 14.8 cm
Collection of the artist

[p. 22] Left: 19/2002, 2002
Right: 9/2002, 2002
Both: Ballpoint pen on paper, 22.4 × 14.8 cm
Courtesy Galerie Barbara Seiler, Zurich

[p. 23] Left: 20/2002, 2002
Right: 22/2002, 2002
Both: Ballpoint pen on paper, 22.4 × 14.8 cm
Courtesy Galerie Barbara Seiler, Zurich

[p. 24] 132/2003, 2003
Ballpoint pen on paper, 22.4 × 14.8 cm
Collection of the artist

[p. 25] 163/2003, 2003
Negro pencil and pencil on paper, 21.2 × 14 cm
Collection of the artist

[p. 26] Left: 176/2003, 2003
Pencil on paper, 21.2 × 14 cm
Private collection, Ghent
Right: 186/2003, 2003
Ballpoint pen and felt-tip pen on paper, 21.2 × 14 cm
Courtesy the artist

[p. 27] Top: 258/2004, 2004
Pencil on paper, 21.2 × 14 cm
Private collection, Ghent
Bottom: 337/2006, 2006
Pencil and colored pencil on paper, 21.2 × 14.5 cm
Collection S.M.A.K., Ghent

[p. 28] 266/2004, 2004
Pencil and ballpoint pen on paper, 21.2 × 14 cm
Private collection, Switzerland

[p. 29] 326/2006, 2006
Pencil on paper, 21.2 × 14.1 cm
Collection of the artist

[p. 31] 324/2006, 2006
Pencil and chalk on paper, 21.2 × 14.5 cm
Private collection

[p. 32] 358/2007, 2007
Pencil on paper, 21.2 × 14.5 cm
Private collection, Munich

[p. 33] 368/2007, 2007
Pencil on paper, 21.2 × 14.5 cm
Private collection, Ghent

[p. 34] Left: 384/2008, 2008
Pencil on paper, 21.2 × 14.5 cm
Right: 385/2008, 2008
Colored pencil and pencil on paper, 21.2 × 14.5 cm
Both: Private collection, Brussels

[p. 35] Top: 372/2008, 2008
Stamp and pencil on paper, 21.2 × 14.5 cm
Courtesy Galerie Zink, Berlin
Bottom: 566/2012, 2012
Stamp, felt-tip pen, and pencil on paper, 21.2 × 14.5 cm
Courtesy Galerie Barbara Seiler, Zurich

[p. 36] 411/2008, 2008
Pencil, colored pencil, and felt-tip pen on paper, 21.2 × 14.5 cm
Collection Kunstmuseum St.Gallen, permanent loan from a private collection

[p. 37] 410/2008, 2008
Pencil on paper, 21.2 × 14.5 cm
Private collection, Belgium

[p. 38] 463/2009, 2009
Pencil on paper, 21.2 × 14.5 cm
Private collection, Mannheim

[p. 39] 403/2008, 2008
Pencil on paper, 21.2 × 14.5 cm
Private collection, Brussels

[p. 40] Left: 374/2008, 2008
Colored pencil and pencil on paper, 21.2 × 14.5 cm
Right: 376/2008, 2008
Pencil on paper, 21.2 × 14.5 cm
Both: Private collection, Belgium

[p. 41] Left: 462/2009, 2009
Pencil on paper, 21.2 × 14.5 cm
Courtesy Galerie Zink, Berlin
Right: 422/2009, 2009
Pencil on paper, 21.2 × 14.5 cm
Private collection, Madrid

[p. 42] 477/2010, 2010
Pencil on paper, 21.2 × 14.5 cm
Private collection, Belgium

[p. 43] 489/2010, 2010
Pencil on paper, 21.2 × 14.5 cm
Collection Kunstmuseum St.Gallen, permanent loan from a private collection

[p. 44] Top left: NR.4(SISYPHOS), 2012
Oil stick on print, mounted on cardboard, 78 × 117 cm
Top right: NR.8(BEANTE), 2012
Oil stick, stamp, envelope, pencil, and sealing wax on print, mounted on cardboard, 117 × 78 cm
Bottom left: NR.3(WERK-KRAFT), 2012
Oil stick on print, mounted on cardboard, 117 × 78 cm
Bottom right: NR.7(PAWLOW), 2012
Oil stick and colored pencil on print, mounted on cardboard, 121 × 81 cm
Courtesy Galerie Barbara Seiler, Zurich

[p. 45] WERK STATT WERK, installation views, Galerie Barbara Seiler, Zurich, 2012

[p. 46] STECHKARTE (POESIE DER LANGEWEILE), 2010
Oil stick and pencil on paper, 179.7 × 119.7 cm
Courtesy Galerie Barbara Seiler, Zurich

[p. 47] FICTIORY (POESIE DER LANGEWEILE), 2010
Oil stick and pencil on paper, 175 × 119.8 cm
Collection Musée Jenisch Vevey

[p. 48] Left: 493/2010, 2010
Time card, ink, stamp, pencil, and felt-tip pen on paper, 21.2 × 14.5 cm
Zeller/Schaefer Collection, Zurich
Right: 500/2010, 2010
Photograph, ballpoint pen, and pencil on paper, 21.2 × 14.5 cm
Collection Kunstmuseum St.Gallen, permanent loan from a private collection

[p. 49] Left: BUREAUCRATIE (0-99 JAAR), 2011
Stamp, ink, chalk, pencil, and colored pencil on paper, 180 × 120 cm
Courtesy Galerie Zink, Berlin
Right: ABSURD HERO#1 (POESIE DER LANGEWEILE), 2010
Oil stick and graphite on paper, 175 × 119.8 cm
Courtesy Galerie Barbara Seiler, Zurich

[p. 50] PRODUCTION LINE, 2011
Spray paint and oil pastel on paper, 180 × 120 cm
Courtesy Galerie Barbara Seiler, Zurich

[p. 51] CHEMIN DE LA VIE, 2011
Graphite and oil stick on paper, 180 × 120 cm
Courtesy Galerie Zink, Berlin

Biography

[p. 53] 527/2011, 2011
Watercolor and pencil on paper, 21.2 × 14.5 cm
Courtesy Galerie Zink, Berlin

[p. 54] 506/2011, 2011
Felt-tip pen, pencil, and negro-pencil on paper, 21.2 × 14.5 cm
Credit Suisse Collection

[p. 55] 516/2011, 2011
Ink on paper, 21.2 × 14.5 cm
Courtesy Galerie Barbara Seiler, Zurich

[p. 56] Left: 547/2011, 2011
Right: 549/2011, 2011
Both: Pencil on paper, 21.2 × 14.5 cm
Courtesy Galerie Barbara Seiler, Zurich

[p. 57] Top: 548/2011, 2011
Oil stick and chalk on paper, 21.2 × 14.5 cm
Bottom: 568/2012, 2012
Pencil and oil pastel on paper, 21.2 × 14.5 cm
Both: Courtesy Galerie Barbara Seiler, Zurich

[p. 58] 523/2011, 2011
Pencil on paper, 21.2 × 14.5 cm
Courtesy Galerie Zink, Berlin

[p. 59] 514/2011, 2011
Pencil and felt-tip pen on paper, 21.2 × 14.5 cm
Private collection, Arlesheim

[p. 60] 474/2010, 2010
Pencil and felt-tip pen on paper, 21.2 × 14.5 cm
Courtesy Galerie Barbara Seiler, Zurich

[p. 64] 502/2011, 2011
Ink, stamp, felt-tip pen, and pencil on paper, 21.2 × 14.5 cm
Courtesy Galerie Barbara Seiler, Zurich

Born in 1976 in Ninove (Belgium), Ante Timmermans lives and works in Ghent and Zurich. He is represented by the galleries Barbara Seiler, Zurich, and Zink, Berlin.
www.antetimmermans.de

BIBLIOGRAPHY

- Philippe Van Cauteren, Mirjam Varadinis & Konrad Bitterli, *Ante Timmermans*, Verlag für moderne Kunst, Nuremberg 2010
- Julie Enckel Julliard (ed.), *Voici un dessin suisse–Swiss Drawings, 1990–2010*, exh. cat., JRP|Ringier, Zurich 2010
- *Mapping Proposal for Kunst & Zwalm 2007 [7 Days—7 Encounters—7 Walldrawings]*, artist's book, 2007
- *Mapping The City (Proposal#2)*, exh. cat., Kunstverein Ahlen, Roma Publications, 2007
- Dirk Schutyser (ed.), *KunstNu*, "Portfolio Ante Timmermans," Vrienden van het S.M.A.K., Ghent 2005, p. 36–43

SELECTED SOLO EXHIBITIONS

2012
Kunstmuseum St.Gallen, St.Gallen
Le Gardien de l'ennui, Musée Jenisch, Vevey*
werk statt werk, Galerie Barbara Seiler, Zurich

2011
Zeitvertreib, Benedengalerie, Kortrijk
Architektur der Disziplin, Galerie Barbara Seiler, Art Rotterdam, Rotterdam

2010
Poesie der Langeweile, Galerie Barbara Seiler, Zurich
Poesie des alltäglichen, o.T. Raum für aktuelle Kunst, Lucerne*
Die Wand ist total super#3, Galerie Zink, Berlin
Konstruktion#1, BE-PART/Platform voor actuele kunst, Waregem

2009
Artist in Residence, Open Studio, Zink Gallery Inc., New York

2008
Mindscape, Galerie Zink, Munich

2007
Ante Timmermans/John Pilson, Galerie Zink, Berlin
Mapping (Proposal#3), Ruimte Morguen, Antwerp
Mapping The City (Proposal#2), Kunstverein, Ahlen*

2006
Ruimte Morguen, Antwerp
Galerie EL, Welle

2005
Mindmap, Croxhapox, Ghent

2004
Bored Control, Galerie EL, Welle

2003
Drawings, S.E.A.S./Scharpoord, Knokke-Heist

SELECTED GROUP EXHIBITIONS

2012
The Ambition of the Territory, Belgian Pavilion, 13th Architecture Biennale, Venice*
The Deep of the Modern, *Manifesta 9*, Genk*

2011
Tomorrow Is The Question–Collection Presentation, S.M.A.K., Ghent*
Voici un dessin suisse–Swiss Drawings, 1990-2010 Aargauer Kunsthaus, Aarau*

2010
Voici un dessin suisse–Swiss Drawings, 1990-2010 Musée Rath, Geneva*

* Publication

This book is published on the occasion of the exhibition *The Guardian of Boredom*, Musée Jenisch Vevey, on view from September 8 through September 30, 2012, as part of the Festival of Images.

EXHIBITION

Musée Jenisch Vevey
Avenue de la Gare 2
CH-1800 Vevey
E info@museejenisch.ch
www.museejenisch.ch

Musée Jenisch Vevey

DIRECTOR Dominique Radrizzani
CURATOR OF MODERN AND CONTEMPORARY ART Julie Enckell Julliard (curator of the exhibition)
KEEPER OF CANTONAL PRINT ROOM Lauren Laz
RESEARCH COLLABORATION Emmanuelle Neukomm
CURATORIAL ASSISTANT Stéphanie Serra
GENERAL ADMINISTRATION AND ACCOUNTANT Bernadette Jobin
SECRETARIAT Agnès Duboux
PRESS AND COMMUNICATION Fabienne Aellen
RECEPTION Isabelle Richoz, Marion Lafarge
TECHNICAL TEAM Michel Cap, Dominique Gigante
SECURITY AND RECEPTION David Moro, Fabian Z'Graggen

Thanks to Cornelia Behr, Raphaël Biollay, Jan(us) Boudewijns, Rik De Geeter, Theo De Meyer, Jan De Vylder, Tanguy Eeckhout, Tatjana Gerhard, Katerina Gregos, Rosalie, Léontine and Nicolas Julliard, Mika Lanz, Eliza Lips, Cuauhtémoc Medina, Mieke Mels, Brice Muylle, Natalija Pocuca, Paolo Salvioni, Marc Schepers, Barbara Seiler, Herbert & Lukrezia Seiler, Nedko Solakov, Stefano Stoll, Jo Taillieu, Marc Timmermans, Vid and Egon Timmermans, Sven Timmermans, Jelis Timmermans, Philippe Van Cauteren, Gerda Van Den Steen, Marcel van Eeden, Thibaut Verhoeven, Inge Vinck, Roland Wäspe, Michael Zink, and the museum's entire team.

An exhibition of works by Ante Timmermans will be presented at the Kunstmuseum St.Gallen from November 10, 2012, through March 17, 2013.

Kunstmuseum St.Gallen
Museumstrasse 32
CH-9000 St.Gallen
E info@kunstmuseumsg.ch
www.kunstmuseumsg.ch

KUNST MUSEUM ST.GALLEN

DIRECTOR Roland Wäspe
CURATOR Konrad Bitterli
MANAGING DIRECTOR Nadia Veronese
ART EDUCATION Claudia Hürlimann, Daniela Mittelholzer
ASSISTANT Céline Gaillard
PUBLIC RELATIONS Brigita Zuberi
COORDINATION Elfgard Sedleger, Samuel Reller, Claudia Stucki
TECHNICAL STAFF Urs Burger, Dani Boller, Joëlle Allet and team

Kunstmuseum St.Gallen is supported by Stadt und Kanton St.Gallen, Ortsbürgergemeinde St.Gallen, Kunstverein St.Gallen.

Kanton St.Gallen Kulturförderung | SWISSLOS

ORTSBÜRGERGEMEINDE ST.GALLEN Leben im Grünen Ring

Stadt St.Gallen

PUBLICATION

EDITOR Julie Enckell Julliard
RESEARCH EDITOR Musée Jenisch Vevey
EDITORIAL COORDINATION Clément Dirié
COPY EDITING Clare Manchester
TRANSLATION OF THE INTRODUCTION FROM THE FRENCH Susan Pickford
TRANSLATION OF THE CONVERSATION FROM THE GERMAN Judith Hayward
DESIGN Nicolas Eigenheer/Vera Kaspar
TYPEFACE Hermes (www.optimo.ch)
COVER #4/2007 (FACTORY), 2007, pencil and oil pastel on paper, 110 × 75 cm. Collection Musée Jenisch Vevey
BACK COVER 521/2011, 2011, ink on paper, 21.2 × 14.5 cm. Courtesy Galerie Zink, Berlin
PHOTO CREDITS Kristof Vrancken/M9 (p. 12); Stefan Altenburger Photography, Zurich (p. 8, 44-47, 49r, 50); Lutz Bertram (p. 49l, 51); Ante Timmermans (p. 13, 15, 19); Dirk Pauwels (p. 18)
COLOR SEPARATION & PRINT Musumeci S.p.A., Quart (Aosta)

Printed in Europe.

PUBLISHED BY
JRP|Ringier
Letzigraben 134
CH-8047 Zurich
T +41 (0) 43 311 27 50
F +41 (0) 43 311 27 51
E info@jrp-ringier.com
www.jrp-ringier.com

ISBN 978-3-03764-278-8

A French edition (ISBN 978-3-03764-279-5) and a German edition (ISBN 978-3-03764-295-5) of this book are also available.

JRP|Ringier books are available internationally at selected bookstores and from the following distribution partners:

SWITZERLAND
AVA Verlagsauslieferung AG
verlagsservice@ava.ch, www.ava.ch

FRANCE
Les presses du réel
info@lespressesdureel.com, www.lespressesdureel.com

GERMANY AND AUSTRIA
Vice Versa Vertrieb
info@vice-versa-vertrieb.de, www.vice-versa-vertrieb.de

UK AND OTHER EUROPEAN COUNTRIES
Cornerhouse Publications
publications@cornerhouse.org, www.cornerhouse.org/books

USA, CANADA, ASIA, AND AUSTRALIA
ARTBOOK|D.A.P.
dap@dapinc.com, www.artbook.com

For a list of our partner bookshops or for any general questions, please contact JRP|Ringier directly at info@jrp-ringier.com, or visit our homepage www.jrp-ringier.com for further information about our program.

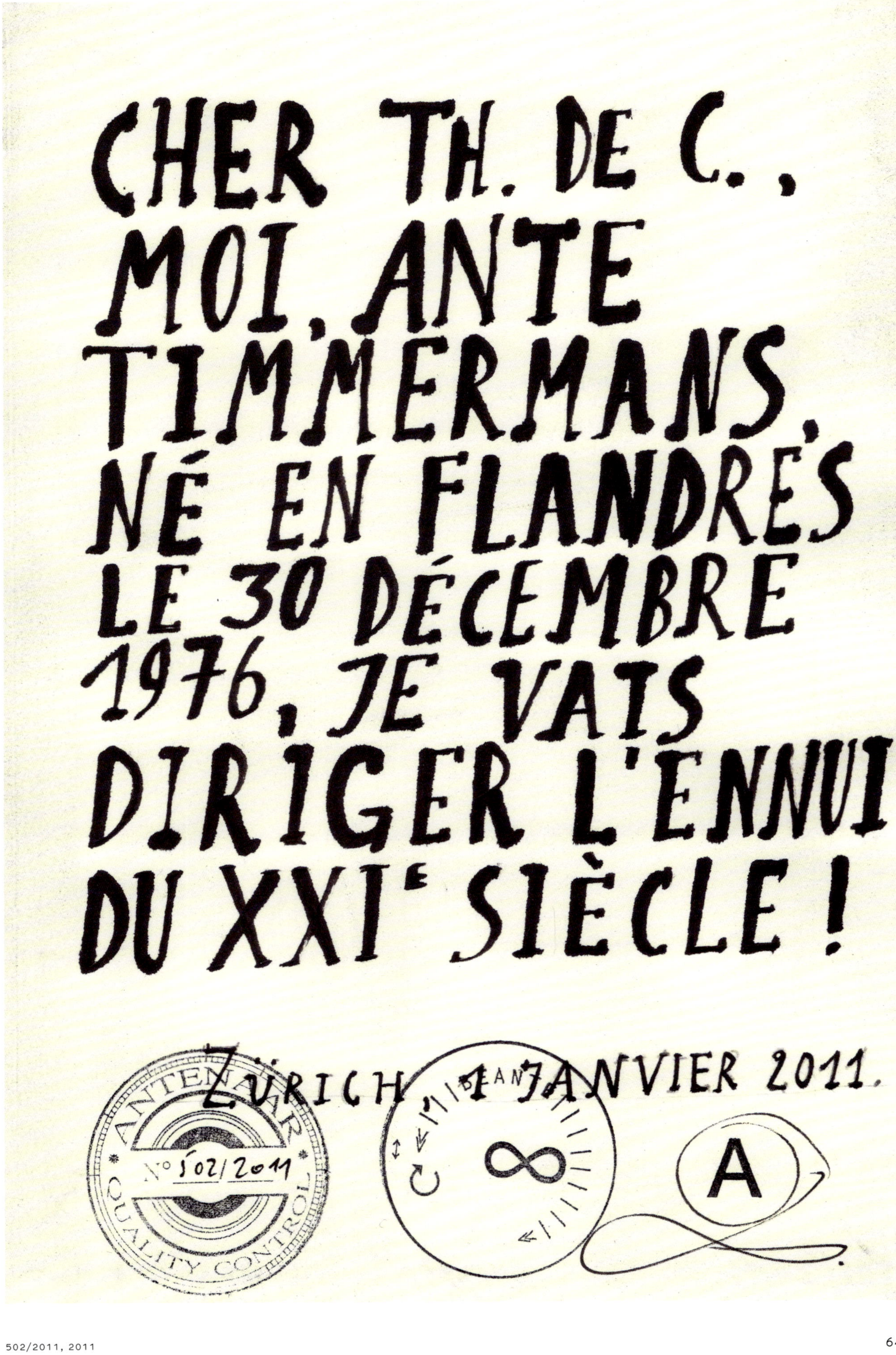

502/2011, 2011